I0831085

THE IMPOLITE CANADIAN

KUMARAN NADESAN

THE IMPOLITE CANADIAN

WHY PLAYING NICE IS COSTING US THE FUTURE

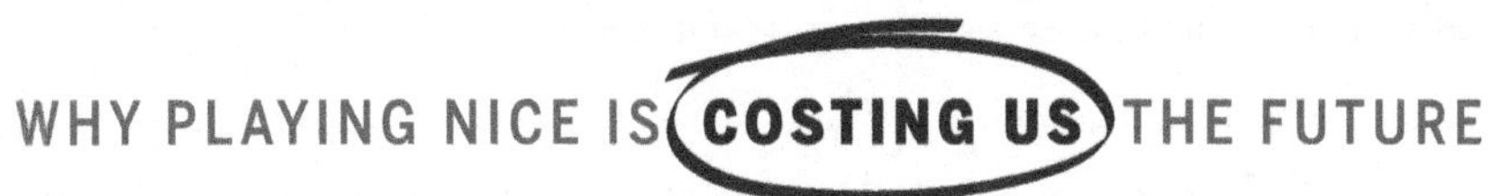

Forbes | Books

Published by Forbes Books, Charleston, South Carolina.
An imprint of Advantage Media Group.

Printed in the United States of America.

10 9 8 7 6 5 4 3 2 1

ISBN: 979-8-88750-740-8 (Hardcover)
ISBN: 979-8-88750-741-5 (eBook)

Library of Congress Control Number: Applied

Cover design by David Taylor.
Layout design by Megan Elger.

01-12-2026 12:38

To Amma and Appa, who taught me that strength can live quietly behind sacrifice and that boldness often begins with leaving everything behind.

To Sahana and Karthik, may you grow up unafraid to speak truth, to challenge comfort, and to believe that Canada can be better— because of you.

To Tharshiga, whose love is my courage, and to my family and friends, thank you for grounding me, challenging me, and standing with me, even when the road became less travelled.

This book is for all of you—the first believers, the enduring anchors, and the silent architects behind this impolite dream.

CONTENTS

PART III: REIMAGINING CANADA'S PLACE IN THE WORLD

PART IV: THE WAY FORWARD

INTRODUCTION

"WHAT DO YOU think of Canada?" This was a question I posed to the head of one of Southeast Asia's largest conglomerates while sitting in his office in Selangor, Malaysia, a couple of years ago. He was an elderly gentleman of Chinese heritage and was only supposed to meet with me briefly. But what was meant to be a quick conversation turned into an hour-and-a-half-long discussion.

Looking at me as if I had just asked the most unexpected question on earth, he smiled and simply said, "I *don't* think of Canada."

Being the cofounder of 369 Global—a group of companies with business interests in skills training, media, and global talent mobility—I often found myself in situations where I had to define my role and identity in new and unfamiliar markets. As someone overseeing international growth and frequently engaged in market exploration, I had the opportunity to participate in official Team Canada trade missions, exploring potential collaborations in talent mobility and media.

It was in these moments of engagement with decision-makers and seeing firsthand the potential for Canadian expertise to make an impact that I came to understand how I can position Canada outside of its borders. This particular business leader and I covered a wide range of topics, including Malaysia's economic growth, the country's political landscape, and even Taoist philosophy. As we approached the end of our meeting, I wanted to gauge Malaysia's market potential for my businesses, so I asked him what he thought of my home and native land.

Caught off guard, I responded, "What do you mean you don't think of Canada?"

He shrugged and replied, "You are just a branch under the mighty American oak. We know you're there, but we don't really have as much interest in Canada as we do in the US."

His response stayed with me. It wasn't the first time I had encountered that sentiment during my travels, but in that moment, it really hit home. For many people around the world, Canada is viewed as an appendage to the United States or, as some have suggested, the fifty-first state.

Another defining moment occurred on the first evening of that same trade mission in Malaysia. The then–Canadian minister of international trade, who was leading the mission, hosted a reception for the Canadian delegates. During her remarks, the minister pointed out a striking example of Canada's often-overlooked contributions to global infrastructure. She referenced Merdeka 118, a towering landmark in Kuala Lumpur and currently the second-tallest building in the world, after Dubai's Burj Khalifa.

She posed a simple question to us: "How many of you know that Canadians were involved in the construction of this building?" Only a few hands went up. The moment was telling and reflected *Canada's* own failure to recognize and celebrate our achievements. Unfortunately, Canadians often assume that our impact on the world is minimal when, in reality, our footprint is significant, shaping infrastructure, innovation, and ideas globally.

But after living nearly three decades in this great nation, operating multiple businesses, and working closely with many government officials in Canada, I am more certain than ever that we are a nation of consequence and a key player on the global stage. However, for far too long, we have remained passive when we should be bold. This needs to change. In the words of Canadian business leader and the chancellor of my alma mater, the University of Toronto, Wes Hall, "When we use the best of us to help solve problems, it solves a problem for everybody."[1]

Canada is a wonderful nation. It's up to Canadians to prove this to the world. To do this, we must be *impolite*. To clarify, I don't mean being a jerk. I mean breaking through the stereotypes that have plagued Canadians and held them back for far too long.

An impolite Canadian is someone who breaks free from the country's cultural myth of quiet deference and instead leads with boldness, clarity, and conviction. They're someone who speaks uncomfortable truths, challenges the status quo, acts decisively in the face of complacency, and stands unapologetically for Canadian values and interests without losing respect or integrity.

It's embracing boldness, assertiveness, and a willingness to break the mould while still embodying respect and integrity. It's about speaking up for what's right, pushing boundaries, and taking risks rather than defaulting to passive politeness or deference. Impolite Canadians are those who disrupt complacency, drive innovation, and advocate for meaningful change—whether in politics, business, or social movements—while maintaining a sense of fairness and responsibility.

Impolite Canadians are not rude or disrespectful; they have the courage to question, lead, and act with conviction. They are willing to defy norms, push boundaries, and refuse to settle for complacency. They dare to speak up, take action, and shape the nation with bold ideas and unwavering determination. It's my hope that this book inspires you to become this type of person and develop a tribe of fellow Canadians who do the same.

PART I

THE MYTH OF THE POLITE CANADIAN

"We only need to look at what we are really doing in the world and at home and we'll know what it is to be Canadian."

—ADRIENNE CLARKSON (FORMER GOVERNOR-GENERAL)

CHAPTER 1

WHAT IS A REAL CANADIAN?

I REMEMBER BACKPACKING through two dozen countries just over a decade ago. I wasn't travelling for business or school. Instead, I was staying in motels and hostels, meeting people from all walks of life. And every time I mentioned I was Canadian, the reaction was always the same: "Oh, Canadians are so polite! Such nice people."

Of course, I'm far from the first Canadian to hear this expression. In a 2022 *BBC* article, American author Eric Weiner wrote, "Canadian niceness is pure, and untainted by the passive-aggressive undertones found in American niceness (have a good day, or else!). It's also abundant. Canada is to niceness as Saudi Arabia is to oil. It's awash in the stuff, and it's about time, I say, the rest of the world imported some."[2]

Flattering as this sounds, I've discovered firsthand that Canadian politeness can be an unhelpful stereotype. Few Canadians want to be or are nice all the time. So, how did this myth come about?

There are many different theories. Canadian politeness likely has its roots in Canada's colonial history and societal development. Nelson Wiseman, director of Canadian Studies at the University of Toronto, suggests that Canada's previous subordinate roles under other regimes, particularly the British, may have instilled mannered traits in the population over time.[3] "Although Canada is no longer a British nation," says Wiseman, "these tendencies replicate and perpetuate themselves like a gene."[4]

"What Is a Polite Canadian for $600?"

Perhaps no Canadian has endeared himself to a global audience more than the host of the long-running game show *Jeopardy!* From 1984 to his death in 2020, Alex Trebek hosted thirty-seven seasons of the show and won the 2020 Academy Icon Award at the Canadian Screen Awards in recognition of his decades-long contribution to television and his impact on Canadian and global audiences.

Trebek, who was born in Sudbury, Ontario, became a beloved figure in broadcasting. As the host of the game show *Jeopardy!* for over three decades, he earned numerous accolades for his professionalism, intelligence, and wit. During his acceptance speech, he quipped, "You know that's not a tough gig. You host a popular show for thirty-six years, you get to be known, you get to be liked." Trebek added, "Maybe people think you're a nice guy? They know you're Canadian—ergo, Canadians are nice people, and the country must be a special place. Well, it is! And not just because we're nice."[5]

That last statement especially resonates. Trebek knew just as well as any Canadian that there was much more to Canadians than being nice, polite people. It's possible Canada's politeness could be a deliberate contrast to American brashness, the way some countries shape their national identities in opposition to their neighbours.

A good example of this can be found in the Middle East. We can learn from the United Arab Emirates (UAE), with its hypergrowth mode, or Qatar and Saudi Arabia competing to build the biggest, most extravagant skyscrapers. Then there's Oman, where I also spent part of my life growing up. Its leaders, especially under the visionary leadership of the former ruler Sultan Qaboos bin Said Al Said, intentionally chose a different path. When they saw the trend of towering buildings spreading across the region, they redoubled their efforts to preserve their cultural heritage. They even passed a law limiting buildings to five stories to maintain their nation's traditional architectural identity.

Maybe Canada's politeness myth followed a similar trajectory. Perhaps, in an effort to distinguish ourselves from Americans, we leaned into the image of being the polite, accommodating neighbour. Regardless of the exact reason, I believe there are three key factors that have profoundly shaped our nation.

FACTOR #1: WE ARE A TRULY DIVERSE NATION

I'll get into this in more detail in a later chapter, but it's clear the demographics in Canada are shifting dramatically. By 2041, 52.4 per cent of the Canadian population is projected to be immigrants or children of immigrants born in Canada.[6] The racialized population in Canada is expected to grow significantly, potentially reaching 38.2 per cent to 43 per cent of the total population by 2041.[7] And by this same year, it's projected that "four out of five Torontonians will be foreign-born or born to immigrant parents."[8]

Of course, these immigration trends are nothing new. Canada has long been shaped by the movement of people from all over the world. Indigenous communities have stewarded this land for millennia, and waves of newcomers—whether early European settlers or more recent immigrants from East, South and Southeast Asia, and Africa and the Caribbean—have each contributed to the country's evolving identity. The challenges may have changed, but resilience runs through as the common thread.

Building a life here has always required grit, resourcefulness, and determination. Perhaps the idea that Canadians are inherently polite was never the full story. Instead, we are a nation of hardworking, industrious people, with each generation bringing new energy and different perspectives to what it means to call Canada home.

Immigrating to Canada and arriving in Scarborough, a suburb just outside of downtown Toronto, in my midteens, I never really saw politeness as a defining trait of Canada. Instead, what I saw in the Tuxedo Court complex where I lived was a lot of grit, hustle, and doing what you had to do to make it in a new country. People were focused on taking public transit to work, saving enough money to finally afford a home, or doing whatever they could to provide a better life for their families. Maybe that's because Scarborough itself is a microcosm of different cultures colliding. When you're part of an immigrant community, just trying to build a life, there's not much time for pro forma politeness. You are respectful yet direct, and you do what needs to be done.

It's clear to me that multiculturalism is a strength, and our nation is better for it. But where I think the conversation gets a little skewed is in how we define and discuss it. Too often, multiculturalism is treated as a surface-level concept, a feel-good exercise in ensuring we see a diverse range of faces in advertising or in corporate brochures.

That kind of performative inclusion misses the point entirely. Representation does matter, but the real question should be this: How are we actually harnessing the talents, skills, and global connectivity that multicultural communities have brought with them to Canada?

This is something I've been thinking about more intentionally over the past few years. Canada's greatest resource isn't energy, potash, or grains—it's people. That said, we've barely scratched the surface of how we could be leveraging our population to strengthen trade relationships, build our soft power, and increase our global competitiveness. We talk about multiculturalism as an abstract good, but are we truly integrating it into our economic, trade, and political strategies?

Canada's greatest resource isn't energy, potash, or grains—it's people.

To me, real multiculturalism isn't about making sure a Tim Hortons ad includes a Black, Brown, and Asian person watching a neighbourhood game of hockey on an ice pond, smiling over a cup of coffee. The real power of multiculturalism lies in how we use it to build a stronger, more dynamic Canada, not in how we superficially display it. What racialized and immigrant communities ultimately want isn't just to see themselves represented in a commercial but to have meaningful opportunities to contribute and thrive.

FACTOR #2: WE ARE A NATION OF DIFFERENT GENERATIONAL VIEWPOINTS

When I interact with older people of European descent whose families have been in Canada for a few generations, I notice a certain benevolence in how they view immigration and diversity. There is a well-intentioned sentiment of "Welcome to Canada; we're happy to have you here," and I don't doubt the sincerity behind it. Many of these individuals remind me of my own grandparents—kind, gracious, genuinely good-hearted. But at the same time, there's an underlying tone that can be grating. It sometimes carries a missionary-like zeal, as if racialized immigrants should be grateful for being accepted into Canada rather than being seen as full participants in building the country.

Part of this is endearing. Canada, after all, was settled and shaped by waves of immigrants, first predominantly white or white-passing, later more racially diverse. With the exception of groups such as the Sikhs and Chinese, who played foundational roles in building infrastructure such as the railways, most early immigration to Canada was framed in a Eurocentric context. So, when older white Canadians express this kind of benevolence, it comes from an ingrained narrative of "We are welcoming you into our country" rather than "We are all building this country together." For younger racialized Canadians, that distinction can sometimes feel condescending or out of touch with modern realities.

Interestingly, when I speak with older non-white Canadians, the sentiment shifts from benevolence to something more protective, almost defensive. Many of them hold Canada in the highest regard, viewing it as a place that provided them with opportunities they might not have had elsewhere. Because of this, they often question why newer immigrants don't seem to appreciate Canada in the same way they do.

I remember sitting with a group of first-generation immigrants during the Syrian refugee crisis, and to my surprise, they were asking, "Why are all these Syrians coming here?" I couldn't believe what I was hearing. These were some of the same people who, only decades earlier, had arrived in Canada under strikingly similar circumstances—

fleeing war, seeking stability, and hoping to build a future. Within a generation, they had adopted a mindset that positioned them as the "established" group, questioning why others needed the same refuge they once sought.

This speaks to a broader tension within Canada: the idea that once you "make it," you shift from seeing yourself as part of an ongoing immigrant story to a protector of the status quo. But the truth is, no one did any of us a favour by letting us in. Canada is a country built by immigrants past and present, and each generation plays a role in shaping it for the next. The challenge is to ensure that we don't forget that.

Canada is a country built by immigrants past and present, and each generation plays a role in shaping it for the next.

For younger Canadians, particularly racialized ones, the mindset is different. They don't carry the same gratitude-first attitude toward Canada because, for them, this is home. They were raised here, educated here, and feel just as entitled to their place in society as anyone else. There's less of a feeling that they must prove themselves or show appreciation for simply existing here.

FACTOR #3: RURAL CANADIANS HAVE DIFFERENT VALUES THAN URBAN CANADIANS

The third critical factor that shapes our national identity as Canadians is the great rural versus urban divide. Taras Grescoe, a Montreal-based writer, proposes that Canadian niceness is born out of necessity, as people spread across such a large territory needed to look out for one another to survive and maintain sanity.[9] But this is changing.

The 2025 Canadian federal election further deepened the country's urban–rural divide in voting patterns. In British Columbia, for example, the election map showed "a few red dots, floating in a sea of blue," with Liberals winning in urban centres such as Metro Vancouver and the southern tip of Vancouver Island, while Conservatives dominated the vast rural and northern ridings.[10] Political scientists confirm that the urban–rural split is more pronounced than ever; where someone lives is now a stronger predictor of voting behaviour than almost any other factor.

Nationally, the Conservative Party achieved its highest vote share since 1988, securing 41.3 per cent of the popular vote and 144 seats, with overwhelming support in rural regions—especially in Alberta, Saskatchewan, and Manitoba—as well as resource-rich and working-class areas in Ontario and coastal British Columbia. In contrast, the Liberal Party's support was concentrated in urban centres, winning nearly all city ridings in Ontario and urban strongholds across the country.

The urban–rural gap between the two parties reached its widest point in recent history, with suburbs emerging as key battlegrounds. The Liberals' base remained younger and more urban, focusing on issues such as climate change, social justice, gender equity, subsidized daycare, and housing affordability. Meanwhile, rural voters, who make up less than one in five Canadians but drive nearly a third of the economy, continued to prioritize resource development, affordability, and concerns about rural health and infrastructure. Voter turnout increased, with 7.3 million Canadians casting ballots at advance polls—a 25 per cent rise from 2021—reflecting heightened engagement across both urban and rural areas.[11]

While I have only spent limited time in rural areas so far, I can say with certainty that it feels like a completely different Canada. Drive three hours away from Toronto, and suddenly, you feel like you're in another world. The people, the pace, and the conversations shift. And with that comes a natural divide, not just in lifestyle but also in political and economic perspectives.

The issues that matter in urban centres don't always resonate in rural areas and vice versa. This isn't a uniquely Canadian phenomenon, of course. You see it in the US and elsewhere, but the divide in Canada feels particularly stark because of how concentrated our population is in just a handful of urban areas.

FINDING MY HOME ON NATIVE LAND

These three factors are by no means exhaustive, but they are key contributors to our national identity. They also reveal just how far-fetched the polite Canadian myth really is and how it reflects more of the Canada of old than the Canada of today. "Real Canadians" aren't beer-drinking, moose-riding, maple syrup–consuming Anglo-Saxons who live in igloos. They are everyday people who value individual freedom, hard work, and providing a better life for their families.

As is sometimes a peculiar trait shared by third-culture individuals, I've sung more national anthems than I thought I would. I have lived in Sri Lanka, India, Oman, and Australia, and each country demanded a new loyalty, a new anthem on my lips. But beneath the words, I always felt unanchored.

Living a life between borders and beyond boundaries taught me to see through nationalism's masks: how "patriotism" so easily turns to xenophobia, how flags can become barriers, how belonging is weaponized to divide. When you've seen people massacred or treated with suspicion or repatriated for the "wrong" identity, you learn to question every anthem's promise.

Canada hits different. It can be a fair country, but it isn't perfect. Our confederation is messy, contested, unfinished. But after decades of moving, of observing nationalism's dark side firsthand, something has shifted in me in recent years, perhaps now that I'm a father myself. Last year, I proudly put up the Canadian flag at home, and it felt *right*. Not because Canada ever demanded my blind loyalty but because it has earned my honest love.

After years of travelling for work and life, especially in the last decade, I've realized this country's greatest strength is that it makes space for complexity, for debate, for adaptability. And the more I travelled, the more I saw Canada through a different lens. Whether it was political stability, economic opportunities, or the general quality of life, my appreciation for Canada ironically grew the more time I spent outside of it.

And while I still have my frustrations, my critiques, and my moments of wanting to push for change, I know, without a doubt, that Canada is home. Not just in a logistical sense but also in a deeper, more personal way. No matter where I travel, Canada is the place I know I can always return to. And that, more than anything, is what makes it *my* home.

BE THE SAME PERSON AT HOME AND ABROAD

The more I travel, the more I realize that I want my global persona to match my Canadian one. Rather than living as a strong business leader and then choosing to embrace a mild, tamed-down version of myself the moment I fly outside Canada's borders or vice versa, I'm committed to being the same person in all settings.

Again, being an impolite Canadian is not about being abrasive or reckless. Rather, it's about redefining what impoliteness actually means in a Canadian context. It's about speaking our truth clearly and unapologetically, standing for what we believe in, and having the courage to challenge outdated norms.

It's refusing to couch our statements in vague, noncommittal language to avoid confrontation. It doesn't mean abandoning kindness, respect, or diplomacy. It means no longer being afraid to say what needs to be said, even when it disrupts the status quo. It means making sure our voice isn't just heard, but rather, it actually matters. When we take a stance—whether on foreign policy, trade, or human rights—it should be because it aligns with our national interests and values, not because it maintains an outdated, comfortable narrative.

Canada has long been seen as a country that follows rather than leads. It's time to change that perception. Assertiveness is not the opposite of politeness. It's the next evolution of it. And as we're about to see, the cost of not doing so can be great.

"Risk more than others think is safe. Care more than others think is wise. Dream more than others think is practical. Expect more than others think is possible."

—CLAUDE T. BISSELL (EDUCATOR AND AUTHOR)

CHAPTER 2

THE COST OF BEING TOO NICE

CANADA IS NOT held together by a common language, a shared ethnicity, or a single unifying religion. Nor do we point to one definitive founding myth. Unlike other nations whose identities were forged through revolution, conquest, or charismatic nation-builders, Canada's cohesion has emerged in quieter, more measured ways. So, what actually binds us together beyond geography and a passport?

At its core, Canada is a country shaped less by grand narratives and more by the steady work of negotiation. Our national identity has been shaped through a series of compromises. It began with uneasy agreements between French and English settlers, continued through efforts to balance Catholic and Protestant traditions, and evolved through complex interactions with Indigenous nations. Regional differences added further texture, as did the arrival of millions of immigrants who brought new cultures, values, and aspirations into the Canadian mosaic.

We like to think of ourselves as peaceful and orderly, and in many respects, we are. But we have also developed a national character that leans toward avoidance. Instead of decisive declarations or sweeping reforms, we tend to consult, deliberate, and defer. We form working groups and parliamentary committees. We issue acknowledgments. We tread carefully. This temperament has given us a stable and, in some ways, enviable society. But it has also made it easier to delay difficult conversations and sidestep uncomfortable truths.

Canada has often avoided the convulsions that have shaped other countries. We did not experience a violent revolution, did not undergo a civil war, and have not been drawn into widespread domestic unrest. Yet, avoidance is not the same as peace, and restraint is not the same as resolve. A country can stay quiet without being truly at ease.

Our identity has long rested on the ability to manage differences rather than resolve them. This instinct for compromise has allowed us to coexist, but it has also allowed injustice and inequality to persist beneath the surface. Politeness can smooth over conflict, but it can also prevent necessary confrontation. We discuss diversity and inclusion but often fall short of genuine transformation. We honour the idea of reconciliation but too often leave the work unfinished.

If Canada's origin story is one of negotiated coexistence, perhaps its future depends on something more courageous. Not a rejection of dialogue or compromise but a willingness to act when talk is no longer enough. Canada may have been built by people who knew how to avoid war and manage differences. The next chapter, however, must be written by those prepared to face hard decisions and speak uncomfortable truths. Our strength going forward may not lie in our ability to smooth things over but in our willingness to risk discomfort in pursuit of something better.

Lost Identity

The cost of being too nice, put bluntly, is the erasure of the Canadian identity, with Canadians who live, travel, or conduct business abroad seamlessly blending into whatever culture they are part of without ever bringing out the distinctiveness that makes them Canadian. It disappears from the idea, the fame, the celebrity, the patent, the trade policy, and even foreign affairs.

As comedians such as Martin Short have noted, Canadian talent has been a driving force behind programs such as *Saturday Night Live*'s success for decades.[12] The show's creator, Lorne Michaels, is himself Canadian, and many of the most memorable cast members hail from north of the border. Dan Aykroyd, Phil Hartman, Norm Macdonald, and Mike Myers are among the Canadian stars who have left an indelible mark on the show's fifty-year history.

Despite their significant contributions, these Canadian comedians often find their national identity subsumed within the broader American entertainment landscape. The Canadian film industry has long grappled with issues of identity and representation. While "Hollywood North" thrives as a service industry for American productions, it struggles to create and distribute distinctly Canadian content that resonates with domestic audiences.

This dilution of Canadian identity in the entertainment world reflects a broader cultural phenomenon. The cost of being too nice or accommodating to American cultural dominance is the potential loss of a distinct Canadian voice and perspective in global media. As the entertainment industry continues to evolve, the challenge for Canadian artists and creators will be to maintain and celebrate their national identity while achieving international success.

Of course, the entertainment industry is a relatively harmless example. This erasure of Canadian identity and consequently the dilution of its impact and influence is much more serious as it relates to Canada's foreign policy and standing with other nations. For example, on June 17, 2020, Canada lost to Norway and Ireland in its attempt to secure one of two nonpermanent seats allocated to the Western European and Others Group.

Norway received 130 votes, Ireland 128, and Canada only 108—falling well short of the required two-thirds majority. This marked Canada's second consecutive failure to win a UNSC seat, following a similar defeat in 2010 under Prime Minister Stephen Harper. "Canada will now likely have to wait until the 2030s to win a seat at the Security Council table—a three-decade absence."[13] Based on Jocelyn Coulon's assessment of this failed bid under Prime Minister Justin Trudeau, Canada is doomed to fail any future bid if we don't have a clear position on Israel–Palestine or do not treat Africa with the seriousness it deserves.[14]

As an entrepreneur, I've noticed how Canada's cautious approach to economic strategy has long shaped its competitiveness, often with mixed results. A major factor has been Canada's deep reliance on the United States for trade. For decades, the United States has been the primary market for Canadian goods, influencing policy decisions and economic forecasts. The problem with this dependency became starkly clear in recent years, particularly when shifts in US trade policy left Canada scrambling to diversify its markets.[15]

Take the Indo-Pacific trade strategy as an example. Canada formally launched a more concerted effort to engage with the Indo-Pacific region just a few years ago, yet it felt like an afterthought—too little, too late. What if Canada had aggressively pursued these partnerships in the 1980s, rather than waiting until economic pressures forced the issue? Had Canada taken a more proactive and, frankly, impolite approach to global trade diversification decades ago, it might not be in such a precarious position today, trying to reduce dependence on the US supply chain while navigating new trade challenges.[16]

A History of Missing Out

Canada's cautious approach on the global stage isn't a recent phenomenon but rather one that has been addressed by various political leaders in the past. Pierre Trudeau, the country's charismatic former prime minister, was notably assertive, emphasizing a bold vision that contrasts sharply with the more reserved, hesitant policies Canada has favoured in recent decades.[17]

The consequences of this hesitancy stretch far beyond trade alone; they are deeply apparent in Canada's struggles to commercialize its technological innovations. Take artificial intelligence (AI) as a prime example. Canada is home to Geoffrey Hinton, one of AI's pioneering figures, based at the University of Toronto. Yet, the substantial commercial successes derived from AI have been largely monopolized by American enterprises such as OpenAI, Google, and Microsoft, companies that have translated groundbreaking research into billion-dollar industries.

This cautious mentality has tangible economic repercussions. Canada repeatedly cultivates brilliant minds and groundbreaking research but continually fails to convert these assets into dominant global businesses. Consequently, the nation finds itself in a frustrating cycle: creating world-class knowledge but leaving other countries to reap the financial rewards.

A similar dynamic unfolds within Canada's abundant natural resources sector. Despite possessing immense reserves of critical minerals and energy resources, Canada's efforts to develop these assets have been frequently stalled by indecision and political gridlock.

Critical minerals such as lithium and nickel, essential for electric vehicle (EV) and battery manufacturing, present an opportunity for Canada to position itself as a North American industrial powerhouse. Yet, Canada's regulations, inability to reach agreements with Indigenous peoples whose land contains these minerals, and limited incentives have led companies such as Tesla to opt for building their battery gigafactories in Germany and Texas, thereby bypassing Canada entirely.

This pattern of missed opportunities also appears in advanced manufacturing. Despite its skilled workforce and geographic proximity to major markets, Canada has lost significant investments to competitors such as the US and Mexico. Volkswagen and BMW notably selected US locations over Canada for their new manufacturing plants, largely because of stronger incentives and more efficient labour markets south of the border.

Even in terms of attracting foreign capital for infrastructure projects, Canada's passive stance differs greatly from its G20 counterparts. In contrast, Australia's proactive courting of international sovereign wealth and pension funds has been a boon for the island nation. While Australia actively engages global investors to modernize its infrastructure, Canada's approach remains piecemeal, restricted largely to isolated successes such as Ontario's Highway 407[18] or Alberta's AltaLink.[19]

The costs of Canada's cautious approach are significant. In trade, technology, resources, and infrastructure, the unwillingness to commit boldly and decisively has allowed other nations to consistently outpace Canada. If this pattern continues, Canada risks becoming a nation celebrated for innovation but overshadowed economically—a place that generates ideas but lacks the courage or structure to capitalize fully on its intellectual and resource wealth. To truly unlock its global potential, Canada will need to reassess its mindset, embracing risk and boldness as essential ingredients for international success.

The Great North Brain Drain

This brings us to perhaps the most devastating example of wasted potential: something we might call "The Great North Brain Drain." Canada has long struggled to retain its top talent, especially in industries such as technology. A conversation I had with the head of a bilateral tech council highlighted this challenge.

This gentleman had posted a simple message in a WhatsApp group for tech entrepreneurs, asking how many would consider relocating to the United States given the economic incentives and policy shifts under Trump. The response was staggering, with four hundred tech entrepreneurs indicating that they were actively looking to move their businesses south of the border.

Unfortunately, this is far from an isolated phenomenon. For decades, Canada has supplied Silicon Valley with some of its brightest minds, with organizations such as the MAPLE Business Council serving as a network for Canadian investors and entrepreneurs in California. The same trend extends to Hollywood, where Canadian actors, writers, and directors have left an undeniable imprint on the entertainment industry. Yet, despite this massive export of talent, Canada struggles to build global powerhouses at home. The challenge is not just about economic opportunities—it's also about how Canada positions itself in the world.

The rise of initiatives such as Build Canada, a civic platform created by tech leaders to reinforce Canada's presence in the sector, suggests that there is pushback against this brain drain. But the fact remains that Canada continues to lose talent at an alarming rate.

The question is why. Is it simply about economies of scale? A lack of venture capital? Or is it another symptom of Canada's cautious, deferential approach—an unwillingness to take big risks, demand recognition, and create an ecosystem that retains its best and brightest?[20]

Perhaps the most revealing aspect of this exodus is the mindset behind it. Some of these entrepreneurs did not simply leave for better opportunities but did, in effect, choose to "ride out" the Trump presidency in the US, believing that the economic environment would be more favourable there. The idea that Canadian businesses would rather relocate than adapt within their home country speaks volumes about the systemic challenges Canada faces in fostering a competitive, globally dominant economy.[21]

At its core, this is not just about economics; it's about national identity. If Canada continues to let its talent and innovations be absorbed into larger global narratives without staking a firm claim, it risks remaining in the shadows. The challenge is not just to recognize Canadian talent but to create an environment where that talent thrives at home and where Canadians feel that staying and building in Canada is not just an option but the best option.

A Wake-Up Call

Addressing the issue of brain drain requires a balance between personal responsibility and systemic support. While it's easy to question the loyalty of entrepreneurs who choose to relocate to more competitive markets, the reality is that businesses will always move where conditions are most favourable. Rather than blaming individuals for making rational economic choices, the onus falls on policymakers to create an environment where staying in Canada is not just viable but preferable.

What does that look like in practice? It means investing in infrastructure, reducing bureaucratic red tape, and rethinking taxation and incentive structures. Canada already has initiatives such as the Superclusters program introduced in the Liberal government's second mandate, but we need to do more.

Ultimately, if Canada wants to prevent brain drain, it must stay competitive. To avoid being overshadowed in international arenas, it must take more strategic risks. And if it wants to foster a culture that values both civility and strength, it must redefine what it means to be Canadian. The challenge is not just in recognizing these issues but in finding the resolve to address them head-on.

Donald Trump's re-election and his administration's more confrontational approach to trade put Canada in a difficult spot, but in many ways, it was a wake-up call. While the initial reaction from some Canadians was frustration or handwringing over the instability of North American trade agreements, others saw it as an opportunity. Business leaders, rather than lamenting the situation, began advocating for long-overdue reforms—such as eliminating interprovincial trade barriers, an issue that has plagued Canada's economy for decades. Suddenly, there was momentum to rethink long-standing economic structures and build resilience beyond US dependency.[22]

Goldy Hyder, president and chief executive officer of the Business Council of Canada, who was first introduced to me as a mentor during my CivicAction DiverseCity fellowship nearly a decade ago, has consistently pushed back against the notion that North American free trade is dead, arguing that there is still much to salvage. But the response to his comments, particularly on platforms such as LinkedIn, has revealed a shift in mindset among some Canadian commentators who believe the old assumption that the Americans would always act as a reliable economic partner has been shaken, and Canadians are increasingly recognizing the urgency of self-reliance.

This is, in my opinion, a very good thing.

Stop Paying the Cost of Politeness

Likability politics is the silent script that too many Canadian leaders and professionals follow without realizing its cost. The desire to be seen as nice often masquerades as strategy, when in reality, it's more about self-protection than leadership. When our goal is to be liked rather than to lead, we risk becoming inoffensive to the point of invisibility—avoiding conflict, withholding our voice, and diluting our presence.

It's possible to be polite while still intentionally standing for our Canadian identity. Nations such as Japan illustrate this clearly. "In the span of only one month from mid-December 2022 to mid-January of this year, Japan revised large parts of its post-1945 security posture and replaced it with a new strategy that—if implemented—would create a more robust and forward-leaning Japan."[23] This nation has demonstrated that courtesy does not preclude strength. Rather, these qualities can enhance one another. As outspoken Canadian businesswoman and investor Arlene Dickinson writes:

> Canada—this is a country that is great. Not because of what we used to be, but because of what we already are and what we can become. We are a country of builders, problem-solvers, and leaders. We don't need to shout about our strength—we prove it. We have the resources the world depends on, the ingenuity to shape the future, and the stability that others envy. We aren't just watching history unfold; we are shaping it.[24]

The cost of Canadian politeness is felt in everyday interactions within communities, workplaces, and families. It affects negotiations for salary increases, advocacy for change, the courage to speak in meetings, or the pursuit of bold personal goals.

If Canada is to rise confidently on the international stage, we need more of a surge of impolite politicians who are willing to speak up for Canadian interests on a global stage, impolite entrepreneurs who are committed to building their businesses in Canada, and impolite influencers and entertainers who retain a strong sense of national pride and Canadian identity. Not people who are rude but people who are bold.

The cost of being too polite is one I'm not willing to pay. And I don't think it's one you should pay either.

"Canada is not so much a country as it is an idea, in the minds of many."

—JOHN RALSTON SAUL (PHILOSOPHER AND AUTHOR)

CHAPTER 3

GLOBAL PERCEPTIONS VERSUS CANADIAN REALITIES

"OBJECTS IN THE mirror are closer than they appear." We've all seen this message printed on car mirrors, and it serves as a reminder that things are not always what they seem. The same is true of nations.

Case in point, Canada has often been perceived internationally as one of the world's most progressive and humane societies. Throughout the twentieth century, the country cultivated a reputation as a champion of human rights, peace, and multiculturalism. From the world stage, Canada appeared to embody ideals of equality and tolerance. We were a nation of peacekeepers and a welcoming mosaic of cultures.

However, this glowing global perception did not always align with domestic realities. Many communities within Canada, such as Indigenous peoples and other marginalized groups, experienced discrimination and rights abuses that stood in stark contrast to the nation's international image. This gap between image and reality would become a defining theme, revealing the complexity behind Canada's benevolent facade.

On the global front, Canada emerged from the Second World War with an enhanced standing as a defender of liberty and human rights. Canadian diplomats played key roles in shaping the postwar order. In fact, Canadian legal scholar John Peters Humphrey hand-drafted the first version of the Universal Declaration of Human Rights in 1947.[25] A decade later, Canada's former Prime Minister Lester B. Pearson was hailed internationally for devising the first United Nations (UN) peacekeeping force during the 1956 Suez Crisis—an effort that earned him the 1957 Nobel Peace Prize.

These contributions bolstered Canada's image as a principled "middle power" devoted to global peace and justice. In the following years, Canada continued to burnish its progressive credentials. It became the first country in the world to introduce an official multiculturalism policy in 1971,[26] embracing ethnic diversity as a core identity. By the late twentieth century, international discourse often held up Canada as a model of democratic values and harmonious pluralism, a country seen as having "minimal human rights problems" at home.[27] But there was something missing from this discussion.

Not as It Seems

Beneath this international acclaim, the reality for many within Canada's borders told a very different story. In 1914, the *Komagata Maru*, a ship carrying over 350 Sikh, Muslim, and Hindu passengers, was turned away from Vancouver's harbour and forced to return to India, where many were killed or imprisoned. And in 1923, the Chinese Immigration Act effectively halted all Chinese immigration, following years of head taxes and discrimination.

During World War II, more than twenty thousand Japanese Canadians were forcibly removed from their homes and placed in internment camps—not for any crime but because of their ethnicity. And into the 1960s, Black Canadians in Africville, Nova Scotia, saw their community bulldozed under the guise of urban renewal, without proper consultation or compensation. These events are not ancient history. They are part of the living memory of this country, reminders that policies built on fear or exclusion have long-lasting consequences for generations.

Indigenous peoples, in particular, endured systematic oppression under government policies throughout the twentieth century. The Indian Act of 1876 exemplified this disparity. It was a sweeping law that treated Indigenous peoples as wards of the state and denied them rights enjoyed by other Canadians.

Well into the 1900s, Indigenous peoples could not vote in federal elections without forfeiting their legal status as "Indians," a restriction that remained in place until 1960.[28] Canadian authorities also blatantly suppressed Indigenous cultures and freedoms. Spiritual ceremonies such as the potlatch (gatherings that blend ceremony, feasting, storytelling, dancing, gift giving, and social organization) were banned from 1885 to 1951 as part of an effort to forcibly assimilate Indigenous peoples.

The lived experiences of Indigenous communities in the twentieth century and even in the present day in Canada painfully illustrate the gulf between external perceptions and internal realities. Perhaps the most visible example was the Indian residential school system, a network of government-funded, church-run boarding schools that operated for well over a century. In what is now recognized as a form of cultural genocide, approximately 150,000 Indigenous children were taken from their families and placed in these schools over the course of the system's existence.

The stated aim was to "civilize" and assimilate Indigenous youth, but the conditions were often dire. Children were prohibited from and even punished for speaking their own languages or practising their traditions.[29] Many suffered physical and sexual abuse, malnutrition, and disease in overcrowded facilities, leading to thousands of untimely deaths.[30] This policy of forced assimilation, which lasted well into the late twentieth century (the last residential school closed in 1996), remained largely hidden from international view.

While the world saw a peaceful, progressive Canada, Indigenous peoples were living, and continue to live, a very different reality—one marked by loss of language, trauma, and the suppression of basic human dignity. The stark discrepancy between Canada's noble reputation and the lived human rights violations against Indigenous peoples is a sobering reminder that a nation's international image can mask profound domestic injustices.

Canada enjoys a global reputation as a beacon of opportunity, progressiveness, and inclusion—a country renowned for its world-class universities, multicultural harmony, groundbreaking technology, and peacekeeping diplomacy. This perception is not without basis. Schools such as the University of Toronto, McGill University, and the University of British Columbia regularly place in the top fifty of international university rankings,[31] and cities such as Toronto and Vancouver are often celebrated for their diversity. But for many who live, work, and study in Canada—especially international students and marginalized communities—this idealized image doesn't always hold up under scrutiny.

Take the international education sector: Over eight hundred thousand international students studied in Canada in 2023, contributing billions to the economy. Yet, many international students face serious challenges—sky-high tuition, housing insecurity, and limited access to healthcare. A survey at Thompson Rivers University found that over half of its international students struggled to find housing,[32] often encountering discrimination from landlords. These students are sold a dream, only to find the reality closer to what some describe as a "pay-to-play survival game."

Even Canada's famed role in peacekeeping—once a core part of its international identity—has faded. While it fielded over three thousand peacekeepers in the 1990s, today it contributes fewer than thirty uniformed personnel across six UN missions.[33] Symbolic pledges have largely replaced substantial commitments.

This tension between external admiration and internal complexity is Canada's paradox. It is a nation of real achievement and real flaws, where global perception often lags behind or glosses over the everyday realities experienced by people on the ground. Bridging this gap means moving beyond polished narratives toward policies rooted in equity, transparency, and accountability. Canada's reputation has been built on ideals; the next step is aligning those ideals more closely with reality.

Beyond the Clichés

That said, while there are ways Canadian reality does not live up to global understanding, there are other ways it far surpasses it and puts to rest some of the common myths that have plagued Canadians for far too long.

While there are ways Canadian reality does not live up to global understanding, there are other ways it far surpasses it.

As Canadian entertainment journalist Dani-Elle Dubé writes, "Over the years Canadians have been pegged by the world as hockey-loving, polar bear-riding, poutine-eating, toque-wearing northerners who love to apologize and say 'eh' a lot."[34] These stereotypes seem harmless at first glance, even charming, but they risk overshadowing the genuine complexity that defines Canada today.

The Canadian experience is far richer, more fragmented, and more fascinating than these simplified stories suggest. Often, global metrics position Canada as a sort of utopia, reinforcing perceptions of it as a land of endless prosperity and unparalleled quality of life.[35]

Indeed, for many immigrants, Canada represents hope. It's a fresh start in a place seemingly free from hardship. Yet the reality, once people arrive, can be quite different. They encounter complexities such as challenges accessing healthcare, barriers that delay or halt their professional journeys, economic struggles in cities with soaring living costs, or even unexpected cultural barriers.

However, the story doesn't end with these challenges, as there are also compelling narratives that defy global expectations in a positive way. I've observed how Canada is often overlooked as a primary destination for ambitious professionals in the technology sector. While associations such as Kanata North are starting to reverse this trend, engineers and researchers often first envision places such as Silicon Valley, seeing Canada as merely a stepping stone or fallback option.

However, I also see some encouraging signs, which I will get to in later chapters.

My aim is not to portray Canada as uniformly better or worse than common perceptions suggest but rather to bring depth and nuance to how it's understood both abroad and at home. Canadian society, in all its contradictions, strengths, and vulnerabilities, deserves to be depicted honestly and fully. By confronting the stereotypes head-on and revealing both the hidden struggles and the understated strengths, I aim to show Canada as it genuinely is—complex, vibrant, and diverse.

Contrary to Popular Myth

While Canada certainly has its challenges, it remains a hotbed of innovation, economic opportunity, and a high quality of life. International assessments consistently rank Canada among the top countries in the world for livability and opportunity,[36] underscoring how far reality diverges from the notion that Canada lags in technology or prosperity.

In fact, recent data across multiple domains showcase Canada's strengths and dispel the myth that the country is lacking in these areas. Far from being a backwater, Canada has emerged as a place where cutting-edge innovation thrives alongside robust economic growth and an enviable standard of living, making it one of the most attractive places to live and work in the twenty-first century.

Canada's prowess in technology and innovation belies any perception of a country falling behind. It became the first country to launch a national AI strategy in 2017, and it now supports a booming AI sector with over 670 AI-focused startups nationwide.[37] Government and industry investment have poured into this field—more than $2 billion in federal funding since 2017—fuelling an ecosystem so vibrant that Canada now leads the G7 in the growth of its AI talent pool.[38]

The country's tech hubs are flourishing. Toronto has risen to become North America's fourth-ranked tech talent market, hosting 40 per cent of Canada's AI companies and world-class research labs from firms such as NVIDIA and Samsung.[39] Clean technology is another arena where Canada shines. The nation was ranked second in the world on the 2024 Global Cleantech Innovation Index, with thirteen Canadian companies making the list of the top hundred cleantech firms globally[40]—an impressive feat for a country with just 0.5 per cent of the world's population.

The country has become a global hub for AI research, thanks to pioneers such as Geoffrey Hinton, Yoshua Bengio, and Richard Sutton. Startups such as Shopify, Clearco, and D-Wave are putting Canadian innovation on the map. However, because of modest branding, a resource-intensive economic legacy, and proximity to the US, these accomplishments often go unnoticed. In a report released last year, *A Mandate to Innovate*, the Council of Canadian Innovators put it more bluntly and called on the government to "compete head-on with the United States for the best and brightest by making Canada every bit as attractive a destination for innovation investment and entrepreneurial talent as America."[41]

Meanwhile, Canada's biotechnology and life sciences industries are also thriving. Toronto's biotech hub alone employs nearly thirty thousand professionals and contributes over $2 billion annually to the local economy, buoyed by strong government support and billions in recent investments from global pharmaceutical companies.[42] These examples illustrate that Canada is not only keeping pace in advanced industries such as AI, biotech, and clean energy, but in many cases, it is helping to lead the way.

Likewise, concerns that Canada lacks economic opportunities or a strong job market are increasingly misinformed. In reality, Canada's labour market has been exceptionally robust in recent years. In mid-2022, the national unemployment rate fell to 4.9 per cent, a multidecade low not seen since Statistics Canada began tracking monthly figures in the 1970s.[43] This historic low reflected a high demand for workers across industries, and job growth has continued since then.

The tech sector, in particular, has become a powerful engine of employment. Four Canadian cities—Calgary, Ottawa, Waterloo Region, and Toronto—posted the highest tech talent growth rates in North America between 2018 and 2023.[44] Toronto alone added nearly ninety-six thousand new tech jobs in that five-year span (a 44 per cent increase),[45] outpacing Silicon Valley's growth and cementing Canada's reputation as a global tech talent magnet. Beyond tech, Canada actively fosters entrepreneurship and business growth through supportive policies and funding. Venture capital investment in Canadian startups reached record highs in recent years, with over $25 billion invested in 2021–2022 alone.[46]

Despite anecdotes about high costs in certain cities, Canada remains an affordable country by international standards, and its renowned quality of life extends nationwide. It's true that housing prices in Vancouver or Toronto can be challenging, but a closer look reveals significant regional variations and overall cost of living advantages. According to Mercer's 2023 Cost of Living Survey, a benchmark for comparing expenses worldwide, all major Canadian cities rank outside the top eighty most expensive globally.[47]

Toronto, the priciest Canadian city, was only ninetieth worldwide in cost of living, with Vancouver at 116th. Notably, Calgary was even further down, in 145th place, making these cities more affordable than many large US, European, or Asian metropolises.[48] Moreover, Canadians enjoy substantial offsets to living costs through public services. Universal healthcare means residents do not pay out of pocket for basic medical care, and education through high school is free and high quality, all of which contribute to overall affordability.

Importantly, Canada's quality of life consistently ranks among the best in the world. Although younger Canadians face troubling livability challenges, in 2023 The Economist Intelligence Unit ranked three Canadian cities among the world's top ten most livable: Vancouver (fifth), Calgary (seventh), and Toronto (ninth).[49] These cities earned top marks for *stability, healthcare, environment, education, and infrastructure*—factors that translate into a safe, clean, and healthy living environment.

Even outside the big cities, Canadians benefit from clean air, abundant green space, and strong community services. In smaller centres such as Winnipeg or in Atlantic Canada, the cost of housing and everyday goods is markedly lower than in global megacities, yet residents still enjoy the same nationwide healthcare and social benefits. The takeaway is that affordability in Canada is relative and often favourable, especially when one considers the high standard of living that comes with the price tag. The country offers options for a range of budgets[50] without compromising on the comfort and security that define life in Canada.

Beyond economics and technology, Canada boasts additional advantages that make it an exceptional place to live and work. One such strength is education. Canada has one of the most educated populations in the world. Over 63 per cent of Canadian adults (twenty-five to sixty-four years old) have completed tertiary education (college or university), the highest rate among all OECD countries.[51] This highly skilled workforce not only attracts employers but also fosters a culture of knowledge and innovation.

Canada is also known for its inclusive and diverse society. Nearly one-quarter of Canada's population is foreign-born,[52] and the country continues to welcome newcomers at record levels[53]—it admitted 431,645 new permanent residents in 2022, the most in a single year in Canadian history.[54] This openness to immigration brings in talent from around the globe, enriches the cultural fabric, and helps drive economic growth (in fact, Canada credits immigration as a key factor behind its quick postpandemic recovery).[55]

Additionally, safety and stability are hallmarks of Canada's environment. The nation consistently ranks among the world's safest countries. In 2023, Canada was rated the eleventh most peaceful country globally (out of 163 assessed), far ahead of its large southern neighbour. Canadians enjoy low crime rates, strong rule of law, and a stable democratic system with sound institutions. Finally, Canada's rich natural environment and well-managed cities offer a healthy lifestyle: Residents have access to vast outdoor recreation, and urban centres are regularly praised for their cleanliness and green spaces.

Canada today is a country of innovation and opportunity, where breakthroughs in AI and cleantech happen alongside strong job creation and entrepreneurial success. It is a country where world-class living standards are balanced with practical costs and where public goods such as healthcare, affordable daycare, and education lift the baseline quality of life for everyone.

Far from being a land of missed opportunities or prohibitive living costs, Canada is thriving on multiple fronts. For millions of residents and newcomers alike, the reality of Canada is one of prosperity, inclusivity, and an excellent quality of life—a reality that decisively debunks the outdated myths and highlights why Canada continues to be globally admired as a place to live and work.

Not Perfect, but Still Great

As Canadians, we will *always* need to overcome certain stereotypes and clichés. Global perceptions will not parallel reality. Being an impolite Canadian doesn't mean we put blinders on and whitewash parts of our shameful past. Still, it's important to avoid certain narratives that suggest Canada is in irreparable decline and instead recognize that Canada is a vibrant, innovative, and prosperous country with an exceptional quality of life.

Canada is not perfect. No nation is. However, its imperfections do not define it. Canada is a country constantly evolving, learning, and striving for better. A country that acknowledges its past, embraces its present, and builds toward a future full of potential. The real Canada is not just a reflection of its history or its reputation. It is a living, breathing example of resilience, innovation, and inclusivity.

Canada is a country constantly evolving, learning, and striving for better. A country that acknowledges its past, embraces its present, and builds toward a future full of potential.

As we move forward, it is crucial to recognize both the achievements and the work that remain. Canada's strength lies in its ability to bridge gaps, to acknowledge its shortcomings while seizing opportunities, and to build on its successes while striving for greater fairness and prosperity. And you can play a part in making this happen.

The reality of Canada is not a static image but a dynamic force—one that welcomes new ideas, new people, and new challenges with determination and optimism. It is a country not just to admire from afar but to invest in, participate in, and contribute to. Because when we recognize both the myths and the truths, we can appreciate Canada for what it truly is: not perfect, but still one of the greatest places in the world to call home.

PART II

LESSONS FROM IMPOLITE CANADIANS

"Never retreat, never explain, never apologize—get the thing done and let them howl."

—NELLIE MCCLUNG (SUFFRAGIST, AUTHOR, AND POLITICIAN)

CHAPTER 4

IMPOLITE CANADIANS WHO SHAPED OUR NATION

CANADA HAS A proud heritage of impolite Canadians. Throughout Canadian history, these individuals have defied convention, challenged the status quo, and ultimately shaped the direction of the country.

These impolite Canadians were bold thinkers, risk-takers, and changemakers who embodied a spirit of resilience and vision that has left an indelible mark on our politics, businesses, and cultural identity. While Canada is often characterized by its politeness, diplomacy, and a preference for consensus, the nation's greatest advancements have frequently stemmed from the efforts of those who dared to stand apart, question accepted norms, and pursue a vision that others could not yet see.

From the early days of confederation to the modern era, Canada has been propelled forward by disruptors who saw *opportunity* where others saw *obstacles*. Political leaders who pushed against the grain, entrepreneurs who transformed industries, and artists and writers who reshaped narratives. These figures remind us that progress often comes not from compliance but from the courage to challenge what is.

The spirit of the impolite Canadian is not a recent phenomenon. It is woven into the very fabric of the country. It is found in the fur traders and explorers who navigated uncharted landscapes, the suffragists who fought for equality, the technological pioneers who put Canada on the global stage, and the activists who reshaped our social conscience.

Throughout the twentieth century, a bold cast of impolite Canadians dared to challenge convention and, in doing so, defined modern Canada. These individuals, once dismissed as radical or fringe, paid personal costs for their "impoliteness." Yet, their courage in defying the status quo laid the groundwork for many of the rights and institutions Canadians now hold dear. In a country that cherishes compromise and calm, it was often the troublemakers who propelled us forward.

Impolite Canadians Push the Boundaries

One such trailblazer was Tommy Douglas, a Baptist preacher-turned-politician from Saskatchewan, whose fierce idealism paved the way for universal healthcare. In the 1940s and '50s, proposing government-funded Medicare was highly impractical. The idea smacked of socialism and faced ferocious pushback.

When Douglas's Saskatchewan government launched public health insurance in 1962, doctors went on a bitter twenty-three-day strike to stop it.[56] Branded a radical and even voted out of his first federal seat amid the furor, Douglas pressed on. His persistence paid off: Within a decade, the once-reviled concept of Medicare spread nationwide, becoming a pillar of Canadian identity. Programs first championed by Douglas, from universal healthcare to pensions, are now widely accepted in Canada.

This transformation came at a price: Douglas weathered being mocked as "Red Tommy" and vilified by the medical establishment. But without his impolite refusal to accept that healthcare was a privilege for the few and not a right for all, Canada might not today boast a system that is the envy of the world. His legacy reminds us that social progress often begins with a lone voice daring to say, "This isn't right."

Around the same time, Viola Desmond was waging a quieter rebellion with seismic effects. In 1946, this Black businesswoman from Nova Scotia refused to leave a whites-only seat in a segregated movie theatre *nine years before* Rosa Parks famously defied bus segregation in Alabama.[57] For her act of civil disobedience, Desmond was dragged out, jailed overnight, and convicted of a trivial tax violation (for a one-cent difference in ticket price). In an era when deference was expected, Desmond's insistence on her dignity was shockingly impolite to the powers that be. She appealed her conviction, enduring stress and public scrutiny, but the courts brushed her aside.

Desmond died in 1965 with little recognition. Her stand was largely overlooked for decades, even though it helped ignite Canada's civil rights movement and led to Nova Scotia ending legal segregation by 1954. It took sixty-four years for an official apology. In 2010, the Nova Scotia government pardoned her, acknowledging the injustice. Today, Viola Desmond is hailed as a civil rights pioneer and even adorns Canada's ten-dollar bill, a face once considered too impolite for the cinema now honoured as a symbol of justice.

Her story illustrates the heavy cost of speaking up in an unjust system: arrest, humiliation, and a legacy that only materialized long after her time. It is precisely because of impolite Canadians such as

Desmond that Canada began to confront its own racial segregation and move toward greater equality.

There have also been moments when Canadian leaders rejected the path of least resistance and chose conviction over comfort. One such example is former Prime Minister Brian Mulroney's unapologetic push for the Canada–United States Free Trade Agreement in 1988. At the time, the idea of linking Canada's economic fate so closely with the United States sparked fierce national debate, with critics warning of cultural erosion and loss of sovereignty. Yet, Mulroney pressed forward, framing free trade as essential for Canada's long-term competitiveness.

He staked his political future on it, calling a federal election to secure a public mandate and ultimately winning. It was a gutsy and polarizing move but one that reshaped the Canadian economy and set the stage for NAFTA. That kind of impolite leadership—decisive, risky, and driven by belief rather than polls—remains a rare but necessary force in shaping the country's future.

Impolite Canadians Pay the Price

Not all impolite Canadians marched in protests. Some worked through high office, bending the machinery of state against the prevailing winds. Pierre Elliott Trudeau, arguably Canada's most famous iconoclast, did both.

When Trudeau swept to power in 1968 amid "Trudeaumania," his flair and intellect were a jolt to Ottawa's clubby norms. As prime minister, Trudeau prided himself on reason over passion and wasn't afraid to behave impolitely on the world stage if it meant asserting Canadian values. He vastly expanded Canadians' civil rights by repatriating the Canadian constitution from British authority in 1982, which included enshrining the Canadian Charter of Rights and Freedoms that empowered courts to protect individual liberties.

But Trudeau also drew outrage for his uncompromising actions. In 1970, facing a Quebec terrorist kidnapping, he invoked the War Measures Act, effectively martial law, sending troops into the streets. Civil libertarians cried foul, and even allies such as Tommy Douglas decried the suspension of rights. Trudeau, unbowed, famously retorted, "Just watch me," when asked how far he'd go.[58] Hundreds were arrested without charge. It was an extreme, polarizing step and one that solidified him as a divisive figure. Yet, many credit it with crushing a violent separatist threat. On another front, Trudeau championed a vision of a sovereign Canada charting its own course distinct from American dominance.

He welcomed American draft resisters during the Vietnam War and provocatively forged friendships with leaders such as Cuba's Fidel Castro and China's Zhou Enlai, years before Washington dared to do the same. These moves were daring, even impudent, in Cold War geopolitics, but they asserted Canada's independent voice. For all his controversy, Trudeau's once-radical ideas—that Canada could be officially bilingual, multicultural, and constitutionally committed to rights—are now core to our national character.

He showed that even at the highest levels, progress requires challenging the polite consensus. Western Canadians vilified him for economic policies, and pundits warned he'd overstayed his welcome by 1984. Still, Trudeau's bold reimagining of Canada endures, proving that shaking up the status quo can leave a country stronger and more itself.

Equally impassioned was Elsie MacGill, a pioneer who broke barriers not in parliament but in the engineering workshop. In the 1930s and '40s, MacGill became the world's first female aircraft designer, earning the nickname "Queen of the Hurricanes" for her role in producing fighter planes during WWII. In an era when women were expected to be quietly domestic, MacGill's very career was a rebuke to polite society's limits. She refused to be relegated to traditional roles, even after contracting polio, continuing to walk with canes and design aircraft with uncompromising skill.[59]

As the only woman in male-dominated factories, MacGill endured patronizing attitudes and stereotypes. (One company grudgingly accepted a female engineer but forced her out when she dared to marry a coworker, deeming a married woman "unsuitable" for the job.) After the war, MacGill turned her trailblazing energy to advocacy, becoming an outspoken feminist and chairing the Royal Commission on the Status of Women in the late 1960s. She had seen firsthand that talent and grit were not enough to guarantee women equality; the very structures had to change.

MacGill's reports and activism pushed for childcare, pay equity, and equal opportunity in education and work—ideas that many men in power at the time found threatening or unnecessary. Her insistence that women be heard and taken seriously was, to some, the height of impropriety. But MacGill framed the women's movement as "part of a much larger … social revolution that carries humanity forward in a great ongoing liberating wave."[60]

Thanks in part to her impolite perseverance, reforms slowly opened doors that young Canadian women walk through today. MacGill hoped to be remembered not just for airplanes but as an "advocate for the rights of women and children"[61]—and indeed she is. Her legacy lives on in every Canadian female engineer. It took a special boldness to live that truth in her time.

Impolite Canadians Are the Architects of Tomorrow

As Canada entered the twenty-first century, new frontiers demanded new impolite Canadians. The realm of technology, for example, was shaped by a quiet iconoclast: Geoffrey Hinton, a British Canadian computer scientist who bucked orthodox thinking in AI. In the 1980s and 1990s, when most experts abandoned neural networks as a dead-end approach to AI, Hinton stubbornly kept the faith. Peers thought his ideas of simulating the human brain were "crazy" and his research path quixotic.[62]

Funding was scarce and career prospects uncertain for someone so far outside the mainstream. Yet, Hinton persisted for decades, tinkering with algorithms that few others believed in. His reward for this impoliteness to conventional wisdom came much later: By the 2010s, neural networks triggered a revolution in AI, and Hinton's once-radical ideas became the new orthodoxy. Dubbed the "Godfather of AI," he was finally recognized with computing's highest honours.

Hinton's story is a testament to the creative friction that impolite Canadians generate. By refusing to go with the flow, he helped birth an industry that is transforming the world.[63] But true to form, even triumph did not tame his independent streak. In 2023, at age seventy-five, Hinton made waves again by resigning from a leading role at Google to speak out on the risks of the very AI he pioneered. He warned that AI systems could spawn dangerous misinformation and even threaten humanity's long-term safety.[64]

Many in the tech elite were startled by this esteemed figure essentially breaking rank—an almost impolite move in a sector enamoured with optimism—but Hinton felt a moral duty to challenge complacency. His willingness to critique his own legacy underscores a common thread with all these impolite Canadians: the conviction that progress without principle is empty. Hinton's unheeded warnings are already sparking urgent debates in tech circles, ensuring that Canada's influence in AI is not just technical but also ethical.

Each of these figures—and other impolite Canadians like them—faced ridicule, resistance, or worse in their time. Their willingness to be unpopular was the price of moving Canada forward. From healthcare to civil rights, from gender equality to national sovereignty to cutting-edge science, they expanded the realm of the possible. They also opened space for today's changemakers.

The universal healthcare system that Tommy Douglas built and the rights that Pierre Trudeau entrenched now empower new leaders to demand even more inclusive healthcare and justice. Viola Desmond's stand against discrimination inspires contemporary fights against systemic racism. Elsie MacGill's legacy emboldens young women and diverse voices entering STEM fields and boardrooms. And Geoffrey Hinton's pioneering innovation, coupled with his ethical stance, lights a path for Canadian tech innovators to shape the future responsibly.

What Defines an Impolite Canadian?

In Canada, being *too polite* often means leaving things as they are. Thankfully, our nation's greatest impolite Canadians refused to do that. Their stories teach us that impoliteness in the form of dissent, disruption, and dogged idealism can be profoundly constructive. Yesterday's impolite Canadians built the stage so today's impolite Canadians can grab the mic.

An impolite Canadian is someone who rejects quiet deference and leads with bold conviction, speaking hard truths, challenging complacency, and advancing Canadian values with clarity and integrity. They go against the grain, not for personal gain or attention but because they see a better way forward. They are unconventional thinkers, unafraid of criticism, and determined to push conversations forward—often in ways that make others uncomfortable. They are not driven by the need for social capital but by an unwavering belief in their vision for the future.

Impolite Canadian leadership should not be confused with reckless defiance. A true impolite Canadian does not simply challenge authority for the sake of being disruptive but does so in service of a greater vision. There is a responsibility that comes with being an impolite Canadian—one that requires both conviction and an understanding of the broader impact of one's actions.

A true impolite Canadian does not simply challenge authority for the sake of being disruptive but does so in service of a greater vision.

A successful impolite Canadian is someone who can be both *bold* and *constructive*, someone who is able to break away from traditional thinking while also laying the groundwork for meaningful change. They must be relatable to everyday people, avoiding the trap of becoming too disconnected from the realities faced by those they seek to lead.

In the Canadian context, impolite Canadians embody a blend of boldness and humility. Unlike the brash Tom Cruise–style *Top Gun: Maverick* success stories, Canadian mavericks tend to operate with an understated confidence. They don't seek the spotlight, yet their impact is undeniable. They are what I think of as "quiet disruptors."

The Cost of Being an Impolite Canadian

While Canada has a rich history of societal impolite Canadians, I am convinced we need many more. One of the reasons we have a shortage of impolite Canadians today is that being an impolite Canadian comes at a cost. While these individuals often lead transformative change, their refusal to conform can carry personal and professional consequences. This is true of impolite Canadians such as Nellie McClung (an aeronautical engineer, disability advocate, and outspoken feminist who shattered barriers in both industry and public policy), who once said, "Never retreat, never explain, never apologize—get the thing done and let them howl!"[65] They embody this spirit of challenging the status quo.

There is always a price for speaking one's mind, particularly in today's climate of social media scrutiny and cancel culture. Expressing unconventional or unpopular views can result in professional isolation, loss of social capital, and, in some cases, active opposition from those who seek to maintain the status quo.

On a personal level, impolite Canadians often find themselves losing relationships along the way. This is a reality I know all too well. The willingness to take an unpopular stand can create divisions, whether in friendships, professional networks, or even within communities. The reality is that challenging deeply held beliefs, even for the sake of progress, does not always win admiration—it can just as easily invite hostility. But Bob Rae, a former leader of the Liberal Party and Canada's ambassador to the UN, once highlighted the importance of challenging the status quo, stating, "The status quo is unacceptable, and it is costly."[66]

Nations are better when they have a mixture of bold, diverse voices. As former Prime Minister Pierre Trudeau noted, "A society which emphasizes uniformity is one which creates intolerance and hate … What the world should be seeking, and what in Canada we must continue to cherish, are not concepts of uniformity but human values: compassion, love, and understanding."[67]

Immigrants Are Born Impolite Canadians

One of the bright spots where I've noticed a surge in impolite Canadian mentality is among Canada's immigrant population. This diaspora has consistently played a crucial role in shaping the nation's economy, society, and culture, becoming modern-day impolite Canadians whose influence can be felt across all sectors.

Recent data highlight their remarkable economic impact. Between 2016 and 2021, immigrants accounted for a significant portion of Canada's labour force growth, helping address crucial labour shortages and keeping the economy vibrant. In fact, immigration is the primary source of Canada's labour force growth, with over 1.3 million new immigrants arriving between 2016 and 2021, contributing to the highest number of recent immigrants recorded in a Canadian census.[68]

New immigrants bring with them perspectives that are not bound by the same social conditioning as typical of those born into Canada's long-standing traditions of deference and politeness. Unlike second- or third-generation Canadians, who may have absorbed the cultural expectation of measured politeness and consensus seeking, immigrants often arrive with a different lens—one shaped by the necessity of adaptability, risk-taking, and directness in their previous environments.

This is evident in the success of immigrant entrepreneurs and leaders who have reshaped Canadian business, politics, and culture. Canada's economy has been increasingly driven by first-generation Canadians who are willing to take risks, disrupt industries, and challenge conventional wisdom. Many of the most transformative businesses in recent decades have been built by immigrants who came with bold ideas and a willingness to challenge the status quo.

There is also much to learn from the political and business environments that many immigrants have experienced before arriving in Canada. In some cases, these backgrounds have prepared them to be more decisive, more globally minded, and less constrained by the fear of breaking with tradition. If Canada is to cultivate more impolite Canadians, it may need to look toward the experiences and leadership styles of its immigrant communities.

Immigrant-led small and medium-sized enterprises (SMEs) continue to punch above their weight in international markets. They have a stronger international presence, exporting more and generating significant revenue from global markets, which in turn boosts Canada's international trade profile. In 2024, Canadian exports rose by 1.9 per cent to $997 billion, while imports rose by 2.9 per cent, exceeding $1 trillion for the first time. Seventy-five per cent of the rise in exports comes from immigrant-run SMEs, "which increased in number as well as in their tendency to export."[69] Additionally, immigrant SME leaders tend to be more educated and report higher rates of technology adoption than their Canadian-born counterparts.[70]

Innovation and entrepreneurship in Canada are also significantly influenced by immigrants, who bring fresh perspectives, diverse experiences, and a robust entrepreneurial spirit. Their contributions have been especially evident in the tech sector, where immigrant-founded startups and initiatives regularly push the boundaries of innovation. Over 30 per cent of Canada's tech workforce is foreign-born, highlighting the reliance on immigrant talent to fill critical gaps in the labour market.[71] This creativity and ambition have solidified Canada's reputation as a global hub for technological advancement and entrepreneurship.

Artists, musicians, writers, and performers from diverse backgrounds are continuously reshaping Canada's cultural landscape, introducing new artistic expressions and perspectives that celebrate and promote multiculturalism. Over eighty thousand immigrants work in professional and technical occupations within arts and culture, with more than three thousand businesses in this sector owned by immigrants.[72] These contributions not only enhance Canada's cultural richness but also foster deeper social cohesion and mutual understanding among its diverse population.

Education is another area significantly impacted by immigrants, especially through international students. In 2022, international students spent approximately $37.3 billion on tuition, accommodations, and other expenses, which translated into a $30.9 billion contribution to Canada's GDP, representing about 1.2 per cent of the total GDP.[73] This economic impact underscores the vital role international students play in enriching Canadian campuses and providing substantial economic benefits.

Collectively, these diverse contributions illustrate that immigrants in Canada are not only key drivers of the present economy and innovation but are also instrumental in shaping Canada's future. They are the impolite Canadians of the present and the future.

How Can You Channel Your Inner Impolite Canadian?

Perhaps you're someone who is a bit of an impolite Canadian yourself. But you've fallen into the trap of allowing your voice to be silent. You've bought into the "polite Canadian" myth and pulled back when you should move forward. If this is where you find yourself today, I challenge you to become bolder.

One of the key challenges impolite Canadians face as they grow older is the balance between maintaining their boldness and protecting what they have built. The temptation to pull back, to hedge opinions, and to conform can grow stronger as personal and financial stakes increase.

There is an old saying that suggests younger people lean idealistic, while older generations become more pragmatic. This pattern plays out in politics, business, and activism. A young entrepreneur may be willing to take radical risks, but as their business matures, they may become more cautious, fearing what they could lose. A bold political leader may start out shaking the system but later find themselves more focused on maintaining stability.

However, there is also a counterargument. Some leaders become more outspoken with time, not less. As they gain financial security, political influence, or social capital, they may feel more emboldened to push their ideas forward. Figures such as Jim Balsillie (former co-CEO of BlackBerry), who has increasingly spoken out on economic nationalism, or Wes Hall (Bay Street entrepreneur and founder of Kingsdale Advisors), who has taken a strong stance on diversity and inclusion in corporate Canada, are examples of individuals who have used their accumulated influence to take stronger, not weaker, positions.

The challenge for you, then, is to continue embracing your impolite Canadian instincts. If you've built businesses, gained political influence, or established cultural credibility, you don't just have the *freedom* but also carry the *responsibility* to lead boldly. Your voice matters more than ever, and your ability to shape policy, industry, and social norms can create a lasting impact on Canada's future.

Internationally renowned Canadian novelist and poet Margaret Atwood famously said, "A word after a word after a word is power,"[74] emphasizing that transformative ideas begin simply by speaking them aloud. To keep this spirit alive, we must create environments—in education, culture, and business—that reward curiosity, encourage boldness even in failure, and inspire innovation.

Whether in politics, business, or culture, the next wave of impolite Canadians will shape our nation's trajectory, forging paths we have yet to imagine. It is not a question of whether they will appear but rather how we recognize, nurture, and stand with them as they redefine our collective future.

Canadian novelist Robertson Davies emphasized resilience and perseverance when he wrote, "Extraordinary people survive under the most terrible circumstances and they become more extraordinary because of it."[75] This resilience underscores why we must create a society that values bold attempts even when they falter, nurturing innovation rather than penalizing failure.

The true test of a nation's strength is not just in the great individuals it produces but in how well it empowers them to lead. The future belongs to those who dare. Let us ensure Canada remains a country where daring is embraced and where impolite Canadians are given the space to rise.

The true test of a nation's strength is not just in the great individuals it produces but in how well it empowers them to lead.

I'm convinced that there lies an inner impolite Canadian within each of us, and I challenge you to embrace yours.

CHECKLIST: ARE YOU AN IMPOLITE CANADIAN?

- ☐ I question the status quo instead of quietly accepting it.
- ☐ I'm willing to be unpopular or misunderstood if it means pushing progress forward.
- ☐ I speak hard truths even when they make people uncomfortable.
- ☐ I take bold risks for the sake of a bigger vision, not personal gain.
- ☐ I don't wait for consensus when conviction requires action.
- ☐ I challenge authority or convention when it stands in the way of fairness or innovation.
- ☐ I accept that being "impolite" may come with personal or professional costs.
- ☐ I blend boldness with humility, refusing to confuse disruption with recklessness.
- ☐ I persist when others dismiss my ideas as unrealistic or radical.
- ☐ I use my influence—financial, political, or cultural—to amplify needed change.
- ☐ I refuse to retreat, explain, or apologize for pushing boundaries when it matters.
- ☐ I see obstacles as opportunities and act when others hesitate.
- ☐ I embrace diversity of thought and welcome unconventional voices.

- ☐ I stay connected to everyday realities, making my boldness relatable and constructive.
- ☐ I believe Canada's future depends on daring, not deference.

"We can choose to be a country defined by the boldness of our ambition."

—MICHAËLLE JEAN (FORMER GOVERNOR GENERAL OF CANADA)

CHAPTER 5

CONTEMPORARY CANADIANS MAKING WAVES

THE SPIRIT OF the impolite Canadian did not fade with the passing of generations. It remains alive today as a living current that continues to shape who we are and where we are headed. The same resolve that fuelled the pioneers of universal healthcare, civil rights, feminist reform, and independent foreign policy now finds expression in new voices, new contexts, and new forms of courage.

Canada's evolving identity still depends on individuals who are willing to speak plainly, act decisively, and refuse the comfort of silence when something must be challenged. Today's context may look different from the political crises or cultural battles of decades past, but the need for conviction has not changed. Institutions are still slow to adapt, injustices still go unaddressed, and opportunities still await those with the nerve to pursue them.

To be impolitely Canadian in this moment is to carry forward a long tradition, not with nostalgia but with responsibility. It is to recognize that bold thinking is not a *break* from Canadian values but a deep *expression* of them. It is to understand that progress often begins with a voice that does not wait its turn.

To be impolitely Canadian in this moment is to carry forward a long tradition, not with nostalgia but with responsibility.

That voice may sound different now. It may speak with new languages, from different lived experiences, or from unexpected corners of the country. But its purpose is the same. It moves the country forward not by fitting in but by standing up. The task before this generation is not only to remember what impolite Canadians have made possible but to continue their work in new ways and with renewed clarity. The path is open for those willing to walk it.

Across the country, everyday Canadians are taking action with conviction, clarity, and creativity. They are redefining leadership not as something inherited or assigned but as something earned through consistent effort, moral courage, and a deep sense of responsibility.

Technology Wavemakers

In the tech sector, Sinead Bovell is a young futurist who has become an influential voice ensuring technology develops with a conscience. Bovell founded Weekly Advice for Young Entrepreneurs (WAYE) to educate and prepare the next generation for a future dominated by AI.[76]

Far from the stereotypical tech insider, she started her career as a fashion model in Toronto. On set, she found fellow creatives were curious and anxious about how AI might upend their industries. Seeing that conversations about emerging tech were excluding everyday people, Bovell made it her mission to bridge that gap.

She began hosting accessible talks and Q&As about AI, targeting audiences beyond the usual tech bros. Her sessions, dubbed "WAYE Talks," were an instant hit and often sold out despite zero marketing, notably drawing crowds that were radically different from the ones in tech's corridors of power or being quoted in the media. "What stood out to me was [that] more than half [of the audiences were] women and people of colour," Bovell says, "and you just don't see that in tech rooms as much."[77]

Bovell realized *who* leads these conversations matters. She hasn't shied away from the tough questions either. Back in 2018, well before AI ethics hit the mainstream, she was already raising red flags about algorithmic bias and lack of diversity in tech. At events, she would boldly ask questions on behalf of the audience: What happens when the people building AI don't reflect the population? What are the risks if we don't have enough voices at the table?

Years ahead of the ChatGPT craze, she even warned journalists to brace for a future when AI might challenge the very act of writing itself. This willingness to call out the "not-so-great things" about technology, as she puts it, alongside its promises, set her apart and earned her a reputation as a trusted "AI educator for non-nerds" (as *Vogue* dubbed her) and one of Afrotech's "top fifty voices shaping the future."[78]

Today, Bovell is an advisor to the UN on AI and a sought-after expert who still speaks in down-to-earth terms, making sure *everyone* can engage with the future of tech, not just the usual suspects. Bovell's impolite "Canadianness" lies in her insistence that technology serves *all* of society and in calling in those who might otherwise be left out or talked over. In doing so, she's making herself accessible to a broader swath of Canadians who are gearing up to face the future with eyes wide open and voices heard.

Yoshua Bengio, another one of Canada's AI heavyweights (and a Turing Award winner), has likewise stepped into an activist role. Bengio leads the Mila AI institute in Quebec, and in recent years, he has increasingly sounded alarms about the "frantic race" between tech giants to build ever-more-powerful AI. He warns this race could have "harmful" effects, from the proliferation of fake news and deepfakes to longer-term threats.[79]

In early 2025, Bengio helped publish the first-ever *International AI Safety Report* and used the platform to call for urgent global regulation. "Without government intervention, I don't know how we're going to get through this," he told reporters bluntly. For a scientist usually immersed in algorithms, such a political stance is notable. But Bengio felt it necessary. He even voiced the chilling concern that humanity could "disappear within 10 years" if AI evolution goes truly awry.[80]

That isn't a sound bite one delivers lightly. Coming from a Canadian known for his calm, professorial demeanour, it landed as a wake-up call to the world. Together, figures such as Sinead Bovell and Yoshua Bengio illustrate how Canadian tech leadership today isn't just about inventing cool things but also about guiding innovation responsibly, even if that means delivering tough messages.

Business Unusual

In the realm of business and entrepreneurship, contemporary Canadians are punching above their weight and doing it with a flair that's turning heads globally. Across the country, there's a surge of founders who are aligning profit with purpose and refusing to "stay in their lane."

Some are high-profile, such as Michele Romanow of *Dragons' Den*, who championed tech startups when few Canadian investors would, or Shopify's Tobi Lütke, an immigrant entrepreneur who openly spoke against complacency in Canadian tech. Others are everyday business owners turning personal convictions into community impact. Consider the story of Tareq Hadhad and the Hadhad family in Antigonish, Nova Scotia.

Newcomers from Syria, the Hadhads arrived in Canada as refugees after war destroyed their home and chocolate factory in Damascus.[81] Rather than passively accept their fate, they started anew, making chocolates in their tiny new town and giving them out as a gesture of gratitude and peace. The confections were a hit, and soon the family launched Peace by Chocolate, a company built on the motto "One Peace Won't Hurt" and a mission of spreading peace through sweets. Their chocolates (often decorated with messages of love) took off, fuelled by community support and the family's sheer determination.

Within a few years, Tareq went from refugee camp to CEO, even meeting Prime Minister Justin Trudeau and sharing the family's journey at peace conferences. A feature film and book have since told their tale. The Hadhads turned a simple small business into a powerful symbol of what impassioned newcomers can do in Canada—not by staying politely invisible but by sharing their culture and values loudly and proudly.

Mohamad Fakih, the founder of Paramount Fine Foods, embodies that same spirit but pushes it further into the realm of civic courage. A Lebanese immigrant who grew Paramount from a single Mississauga shawarma shop into a global franchise, Fakih has never confined himself to the safe space of entrepreneurship. He has repeatedly taken public stances on polarizing issues, most recently on Canada's response to the Israel–Palestine war. In doing so, he has endured boycotts, harassment, and significant financial loss. Yet, Fakih has remained unapologetic, arguing that moral leadership requires speaking up even when it costs you customers. In a business culture that often equates neutrality with prudence, Fakih's decision to put values before profit is profoundly un-Canadian in the best possible way. It is assertive, confrontational, and unwilling to let polite silence be mistaken for virtue.

Hadhad and Fakih reveal two sides of immigrant impoliteness: the hustle to claim economic space and the courage to occupy civic space. Both men defy Canada's unspoken expectation that immigrants should prove their worth quietly, avoiding controversy for fear of being told to "go back where you came from." Hadhad's success normalizes refugees as job creators, not burdens. Fakih's advocacy challenges the myth that prosperity should come at the price of political muteness. The lesson is not that immigrants must abandon politeness to lead. It is that Canada must broaden its understanding of what leadership from newcomers can look like—sometimes patient and rooted in community and other times outspoken and values-driven but always grounded in hard work, excellence, and contribution. True belonging in Canada doesn't require shedding politeness. It requires the space for newcomers—once they have built their place here—to speak, build, dissent, and lead as full participants in the national project.

Culture Catalysts

Culture is the soul of a country, and Canada's soul is being invigorated by artists and cultural figures who aren't afraid to make some noise. They span the famous to the grassroots, but all share a willingness to challenge expectations. On the mainstream stage, few are as emblematic as Ryan Reynolds. His cultural impact, from proudly Canadian humour in global interviews to making a Canadian song ("Ahead by a Century" by The Tragically Hip) the soundtrack to a Hollywood montage, has reinforced that Canada's voice can be cool, confident, and current.

Another household name, Simu Liu, has likewise broadened perceptions. Born in China, raised in Ontario, Simu went from unknown accountant to Marvel's first Asian superhero. Along the way, he's been a refreshingly vocal advocate in pushing for representation. When a Disney CEO's remark dubbed his film "an experiment," Simu took to social media to proudly assert his worth: "We are not an experiment. We are the underdog; the underestimated. We are the ceiling-breakers."[82]

He speaks often about taking up space as an Asian Canadian and challenging old Hollywood tropes. Watching Simu host *Saturday Night Live* or address students about diversity, Canadians see a new kind of leading man, one who blends charm with a social mission. It signals to every kid from an immigrant family that *their* stories and faces belong at the centre, not the margins. This, too, is Canada now.

But some of the most exciting cultural waves are coming from independent and grassroots creators. Lido Pimienta is one such force. An experimental musician and visual artist, Pimienta was relatively under the radar until she won the prestigious Polaris Music Prize in 2017 for her album *La Papessa*. On that album (recorded in her Toronto apartment), she fused Afro-Colombian beats with electronic soundscapes and pointed lyrics about identity, race, and womanhood.

Yet, it's perhaps what happened after that truly cemented her as a cultural catalyst. During her live shows, Pimienta invites "Brown girls to the front," literally asking women of colour in the audience to come forward and enjoy the concert up close, while requesting others respectfully make room.[83]

It's a direct, impassioned act meant to centre those usually pushed to the back. In one highly publicized incident in Halifax, a white volunteer resisted this arrangement, only to be called out and removed by Pimienta herself for her "overtly racist" disruption. The festival organizers apologized to the artist, acknowledging the racism she faced.[84]

For some observers, this was shocking. Here was a performer setting ground rules that upended the status quo of who gets priority at shows. But for many others, especially fans of colour, it was electrifying and long overdue. Pimienta's stance was that at *her* show, in *her* space, the historically marginalized would be celebrated, not sidelined. It was a profoundly visible assertion of values through art. And it resonated: Pimienta has since toured globally, become an advocate for inclusive festival practices, and continued making fiercely original art.

Grassroots Change and Bold Policy Voices

Not all changemakers need a public platform or a business venture. Some influence Canada's direction through grassroots activism and policy reform. Often, these figures start as ordinary citizens who simply refuse to accept "the way things are." In doing so, they personify the idea that anyone can channel a bit of impolite Canadianness to effect change.

One of the most inspiring examples is Autumn Peltier, a teenage activist from Wiikwemkoong First Nation in Ontario. Autumn was just eight years old when she began speaking up for water protection, and by the age of twelve, she was holding national leaders to account.

In 2016, at a ceremony in Gatineau, this soft-spoken yet steely Anishinaabe girl presented a ceremonial water bowl to Prime Minister

Justin Trudeau, then confronted him about policies that threatened clean water. "I am very unhappy with the choices you've made … the pipelines," she told the prime minister frankly, even as tears ran down her cheeks.[85] Those simple, quavering words and calling out the leader of the country in defence of her people's water reverberated across Canada.

Here was a child doing what many adults dared not: speaking truth to power with heartfelt conviction. Trudeau was reportedly left momentarily speechless, and a "star was born," as media later put it.[86] Autumn has since addressed the UN (at the ripe age of thirteen) as the appointed chief water commissioner for the Anishinabek Nation, carrying on the work of her late aunt Josephine Mandamin (the founder of the water protectors movement). Now in her late teens, Autumn continues to campaign for access to clean drinking water in Indigenous communities, an issue that, shamefully, remains unresolved in parts of Canada.

Her activism has spurred tangible results and put pressure on the government to invest more in water infrastructure, and, perhaps more importantly, it has awakened Canadians to an injustice often ignored. Autumn's courage exemplifies how even a young Indigenous girl can exercise tremendous moral power by being respectfully yet resolutely impolite in the face of wrong. She often says she's giving water "a voice."[87] In doing so, she's become the voice of a new generation of Indigenous youth who are no longer content to be silent or patient about their rights.

Autumn's story is extraordinary, but she is far from alone. Across Canada, everyday citizens have been taking similarly bold action on issues they care about. In Toronto, for instance, a group of mothers outraged by gun violence in their neighbourhood formed a grassroots network to lobby for safer streets and mentor local youth. They showed up at city council meetings uninvited and refused to leave until officials listened. Their advocacy helped initiate community programs that have steered kids away from gangs.

In Montreal, when a borough announced plans to cut down dozens of healthy trees, residents banded together in protest, eventually convincing the council to reverse course and adopt a greener approach to urban planning. In Vancouver, disability rights activists have "hacked" public transit by crowdsourcing a map of accessible routes and then pressing the transit authority to make those improvements permanent.

These might seem like small victories or niche causes, but collectively, they indicate a shift: Canadians are less inclined to say "sorry to bother you" when faced with injustice or bureaucratic indifference. Instead, more people are recognizing their own agency to create change, whether through a well-timed public challenge, a viral social media campaign, or persistent community organizing.

More people are recognizing their own agency to create change, whether through a well-timed public challenge, a viral social media campaign, or persistent community organizing.

A Blueprint for the New Canadian Leadership

From the innovation labs of Toronto to the grassroots stages of indie concerts in Halifax, from corporate boardrooms to climate justice protests, a new kind of Canadian leadership is emerging. It's not polished for press releases. It doesn't come from elite institutions or unfold neatly through hierarchy. It's forged in messy, personal, and often uncomfortable conviction, and it is actively rewriting what it means to lead in this country.

What ties these changemakers together isn't simply their visibility or professional achievements. It's the unmistakable thread of purpose running through everything they do. Sinead Bovell doesn't critique AI because it's fashionable. She does it because she understands how unchecked technologies can hurt people who look like her.

Autumn Peltier doesn't speak at global summits for applause. She does it because she carries the burden of generations who have lived without safe, clean water. These individuals act not for personal gain but from a deep-rooted sense of responsibility. That clarity of purpose gives them strength when the path gets steep and institutions resist change.

And here's the challenge: That same clarity is available to you. You don't need to be an expert. You don't need to be at the top of your field. You don't even need to be particularly loud. You just need to be an everyday Canadian who cares deeply enough about something that you're willing to stand for it, even if your voice shakes. Purpose is not a personality trait. It is a decision.

You don't need to be an expert. You don't need to be at the top of your field. You don't even need to be particularly loud. You just need to be an everyday Canadian who cares deeply enough about something that you're willing to stand for it, even if your voice shakes.

One of the defining qualities of these modern leaders is that they do not simply resist outdated norms. They question why those norms exist in the first place. They reject the passive explanations we've come to accept. When someone says, "That's just how it works," they respond, "Why should it?"

They interrogate power structures, reimagine broken systems, and ask better questions. *Who is included? Who is excluded? Who profits? And what would it look like to build something more just?* This curious, critical, and constructive posture is becoming one of the most powerful traits in Canada's evolving identity. And it's a mindset anyone, including you, can adopt.

Impolite Canadians are not climbing ladders. They are building bridges and bringing others with them. They create platforms, mentor outsiders, share tools, and speak names that haven't been heard before. These are not airbrushed, unapproachable icons. They are real and funny, and they speak plainly, admit what they don't know, share their doubts, and keep moving forward despite the odds.

They are living proof that you don't have to ask for permission to be an impolite Canadian. You can begin today. You, too, can lead. You, too, can question, connect, and create. You, too, can be a wavemaker.

"Canada is the only country in the world that knows how to live without an identity."

—MARSHALL MCLUHAN (MEDIA THEORIST)

CHAPTER 6

THE DIASPORA EFFECT

MUCH HAS BEEN said about Canada's immigrant population and the fact that nearly one in four people in Canada today were born in another country. This represents the highest proportion of immigrants in our history and the largest share in the G7.[88] But what many don't realize is that an entire province's worth of Canadian citizens, about three million people, live outside Canada's borders.

John Stackhouse, a former journalist and one of my favourite authors, frames it powerfully when he notes that our country's greatest untapped resource may be the three million Canadians who don't live here.[89] In *Planet Canada*, Stackhouse argues that members of Canada's diaspora share an instinct to "export Canadian values" and act as ambassadors for Canada in industries and societies where official diplomacy can't easily reach.

For most of Canada's history, we've been defined by who came here. However, in the twenty-first century, something unexpected happened, as more and more Canadians began to flow in the opposite direction. From Hong Kong to Silicon Valley and from London to

Lagos, the Canadian presence abroad has increased dramatically. And with this increase comes influence, identity, and opportunity.

Stackhouse writes, "While Canada's share of global everything—GDP, defence, aid, R&D—has declined, our share of expat influence has grown."[90] In a world where hard power has faded and soft power is currency, our global citizens are quietly reshaping how Canada is seen and what it means to be Canadian.

What's powerful about the Canadian diaspora is not just its size but its spirit. We're not a former colonial power with sprawling embassies or military bases. Our influence doesn't come from conquest or coercion. It comes from connectivity. The Canadians abroad who thrive do so not just by being *smart* but by being *human.*

Our influence doesn't come from conquest or coercion. It comes from connectivity.

"For as long as humans have organized themselves outside the family unit—first tribes, then dialects, then nations—there have been diasporas, and with them diaspora politics."[91] What's changed is that modern diaspora communities are both more mobile and more connected than ever before. "As international travel and the spread of liberty enabled humans to move in ever-larger groups all over the planet," Stackhouse explains, "their governments back home discovered the power of diaspora politics, and with it a need for diaspora diplomacy."[92]

Thankfully, Canada has already laid the groundwork. The 1977 Citizenship Act liberalized dual citizenship, allowing newcomers and outward-bound Canadians alike to remain tethered to the homeland while participating fully abroad. "It told millions around the world they could come here and still keep a bit of themselves there."[93] That flexibility has birthed what Stackhouse calls "a hyphenated diaspora."

This is the new vision of Canada: a nation not just of geography but of global reach. "If Canada is to maintain or even build our relevance in a technology-driven world in the decades ahead," Stackhouse argues, "we may have no greater tool at our disposal than those expats."[94]

A Changing of the Guard

A lot has happened since *Planet Canada* was published in 2020, and our diaspora could be even larger than believed. More importantly, the diaspora is skewing younger and more diverse, with many leaving Canada today in their twenties and thirties. They are well educated, globally minded, and hungry for experience.[95]

They're heading to tech startups in Berlin, finance giants in Singapore, media companies in New York, and they're often achieving great things under the radar. This new wave doesn't have the household names of the previous generation (not everyone will become the next Mark Carney or Louise Arbour), but their impact is tangible in aggregate.

A decade ago, our expat cultural icons were folks such as Neil Young or Celine Dion. Today, you'll find a rising class of Canadian creators thriving abroad in less obvious places. For example, you will find a Canadian journalist hosts a news show in London; a Vancouver-born chef runs a fusion restaurant in Hong Kong; a young Albertan is heading a renewable energy startup in Chile. These individuals might not be famous back home, but they carry pieces of Canada into boardrooms, newsrooms, and community projects worldwide.

In diplomacy too, younger Canadian expats are making their mark. A case in point is the C100 network in Silicon Valley, founded by

Canadian tech entrepreneurs abroad. It has become a powerful engine linking Canada to the world's tech epicentre. It has mentored startups, pushed for fast-track visas, and even helped shape Canada's AI strategy.[96]

What ties these younger, lesser-known diaspora figures together is a shared ease with crossing borders. They are what *3 Magazine* (a new media platform for third-culture Canadians founded by my friend and cofounder at 369 Global, Muraly Srinarayanathas) calls "people who live between borders and beyond boundaries," born in one place but enriched by many others.[97] They don't see leaving Canada as a betrayal but as an extension of Canadian identity. And many fully intend to circulate back and forth.

In short, the diaspora is becoming a two-way street. It's a fluid exchange of ideas and opportunities, rather than a permanent one-way exodus.

The diaspora is becoming a two-way street. It's a fluid exchange of ideas and opportunities, rather than a permanent one-way exodus.

Rebuilding Traditional Tamil Homelands in Sri Lanka

To illustrate diaspora-led development in action, let me share a deeply personal story. After Sri Lanka's civil war ended in 2009, many in the Tamil diaspora (including myself) felt a profound urge to give back and help rebuild. But the instinct wasn't to be confrontational or brash; it was simply to move beyond passivity. Instead of limiting ourselves to charitable donations or symbolic gestures, we wanted to bring the skills, knowledge, and confidence that come from our Canadian experience. In 2016, I cofounded an organization called comdu.it (pronounced "com-do-it") to do exactly that—act as a conduit for diaspora professionals to volunteer in postwar Sri Lanka. We started small, but with a big idea to pair the energy and expertise of young diaspora Canadians with the needs of communities in Sri Lanka's war-affected Northern and Eastern provinces.

This idea was actually born earlier. Back in 2003, during a ceasefire in the Sri Lankan conflict, some friends and I launched The Student Volunteer Program, sending Canadian university students to volunteer in the Tamil regions for the first time.[98] That summer, I found myself teaching English and computer skills in Kilinochchi and helping set up libraries and websites for local communities. It was a life-changing experience. I saw firsthand how diaspora youth, with their blend of Canadian education and Tamil heritage, could plug in quickly and make a difference on the ground. What struck me then was not that diaspora youth were bold or outspoken, but that they were unafraid to show up. They didn't wait for permission, perfect conditions, or an established template. They took initiative. That, in many ways, is the "impoliteness" I argue Canada needs more of—not rudeness, but a willingness to step forward rather than remain deferential or invisible. Most importantly, I learned from the people living with the daily reality of war, gaining insight into how we outsiders could best help. That early experiment planted a seed in me that diaspora engagement could be a two-way street of learning and impact.

Years later, with the war over, we poured new life into that idea with comdu.it. Since its founding in 2016, comdu.it has sent several dozen diaspora professionals from Canada and other Western countries (United States, Germany, Switzerland, Norway, Australia) to volunteer with local partners in Sri Lanka. These volunteers include engineers, social workers, researchers, and entrepreneurs, and they spend weeks or months working on projects ranging from rural entrepreneurship to mental health services in war-torn districts. While our numbers aren't massive, our work has touched roughly 70 per cent of the districts in Sri Lanka, especially the northern and eastern Tamil homelands, building everything from tech training workshops to civic programs. We've essentially created a *pipeline of expertise* flowing from the diaspora back to the homeland.

The impact goes beyond metrics. By having diaspora youth working side by side with local Sri Lankan organizations, we catalyze new ideas and trust. A German Tamil consultant at McKinsey advising Tamil startups in Jaffna, an award-winning Canadian Tamil choreographer working to empower girls in Batticaloa through dance, a Norwegian Tamil engineer assisting with community infrastructure building in Mannar. These are modest efforts individually, but collectively, they start to change the postwar recovery narrative from one of dependency to one of partnership with the global Tamil community. Sri Lankan stakeholders see that members of diaspora aren't just cheque writers living abroad but are willing to roll up their sleeves and contribute on the ground.

Importantly, even governments have started to take note. Our work with comdu.it earned recognition from the Canadian and German diplomatic missions in Sri Lanka and private foundations in the United States, among others. This was encouraging, but it also underscores how diaspora initiatives often operate parallel to official channels. We filled a gap that traditional development agencies weren't addressing—not because we were louder or more confrontational, but because we were more proactive. We didn't wait for government programs or UN frameworks; we moved first. So, when I argue that Canada needs to shed elements of its political and diplomatic politeness, I am not advocating for abrasiveness or bravado. The comdu.it story shows a different kind of impoliteness: the refusal to be passive, deferential, or comforted by symbolic gestures when real action is needed. As I often describe it, "comdu.it is about building a resilient and impactful bridge into the future between the next generation of the homeland and the diaspora—and we don't take that responsibility lightly."[99] This is the through-line to Canada's foreign policy more broadly. Diaspora communities—Tamil, Ukrainian, Filipino, Ethiopian, Jamaican, Indian, and many others—are reservoirs of insight, networks, and cultural fluency. They can help Canada build deeper ties, understand emerging markets, and identify opportunities long before official channels catch up. But that requires Ottawa to see them as partners, not footnotes.

If Canada is to thrive in a multipolar world, it needs a foreign policy that mirrors the confidence and initiative of its diasporas—engaged, unafraid to lead, and willing to step forward even in imperfect conditions. The Tamil diaspora's work in Sri Lanka is just one example of how that shift in posture can look.

From Brain Drain to Brain Circulation

While one might assume Canada has a grand strategy to engage and leverage its diasporas, this could not be further from the truth. The government of Canada does not in fact have an official strategy for cultivating the diaspora,[100] and this, in my opinion, is a glaring oversight.

Other countries have long recognized the value of their people abroad. Ireland, Israel, India, the Philippines, Italy, China, and many more actively court and integrate their diasporas into national affairs. They host diaspora conferences, offer incentives for returnees, maintain databases of expatriate talent, and even extend voting rights or parliamentary representation to citizens overseas.

Canada, by contrast, has been stuck in an older mindset, defaulting to Eurocentric and colonial-era frameworks of engagement. We've historically focused on our relationships with France, Britain, and the US and on formal state-to-state diplomacy while largely ignoring the network of twenty-first-century global Canadians at our fingertips. The result is a missed opportunity of massive proportions. As one Senate report bluntly put it, our diaspora is an "active international community and an untapped resource" for Canada.[101]

For too long, Canadians have discussed emigration in terms of brain drain, as if every talented person who leaves is lost forever. This defeatist mindset needs to go. Instead, we should be focusing on brain *circulation*, a virtuous cycle where Canadians go out into the world and many come back (or stay connected) with enhanced skills, ideas, and networks. By facilitating circulation, we enhance Canada's influence in the world and benefit from the knowledge and experience of all our citizens.[102]

What does brain circulation look like in practice? It means making it easy for Canadians to leave and return. Many of our expats do want to come back at some point, often to raise families or start enterprises in Canada, but they hit barriers. Professional credentials may not be recognized upon return. The job market may not value international experience, viewing a decade overseas as a gap rather than an asset.

I've heard from numerous Canadians abroad who were frustrated trying to repatriate. One had led a major NGO in Europe but struggled to land a comparable role here; another ran a fintech startup in Asia, but Canadian investors were wary because it wasn't North American experience. We have to fix those attitudes. If someone has been working on the cutting edge in London or Singapore or Nairobi, we should treat them like gold, not make them start from scratch.

We should also actively entice the members of our diaspora to stay connected, even if they don't move back physically. This could mean supporting Canadian alumni networks worldwide or engaging successful expats as mentors for Canadian projects. Some countries incentivize the members of their diasporas to invest back home, and Canada could do more there, perhaps through diaspora bonds or matching funds for diaspora-driven ventures.

Beyond policy, a mindset shift is needed: Canadians must stop viewing spending time abroad as disloyal or problematic. In the 1990s, the term *brain drain* was used almost as a scare tactic, implying that if too many left, Canada was doomed. But many who left in that era ended up helping Canada in new ways, or they eventually returned.

Canada can be both a launchpad and a beneficiary of global ideas through this circulation. The circular flow of people means Canada can be a living lab for global innovation, and then our diaspora carries those successes abroad, building Canada's brand.

From Footnotes to Front Lines

No longer can we afford to see the members of our diaspora as mere footnotes, sidebars, or afterthoughts. They are frontline agents of change for Canada in the twenty-first century. In a world defined by networks and mobility, our diaspora *is* our strength. But realizing that strength requires action and attitude shifts.

First, we must value and engage our diaspora intentionally. This means a paradigm shift at the highest levels: The Canadian government should develop a clear diaspora engagement strategy, with input from the communities themselves. This looks like creating mechanisms to regularly consult with Canadians overseas on trade, innovation, and cultural promotion; establishing diaspora advisory councils for key regions; and recognizing diaspora contributions with awards or even representation. These are bold ideas, but the message they send is simple: *You matter to Canada.*

Second, we need to invest in diaspora-led initiatives. When diasporas organize programs to benefit Canada or their heritage communities, support them. Whether it's a group of expat engineers mentoring STEM students back home or a cultural diaspora festival that strengthens international ties, these efforts yield returns in goodwill and global linkages. My experience with comdu.it taught me that a small investment in diaspora-led development can pay off in spades through community impact and bilateral relations. Government agencies, foundations, and the private sector should partner with diaspora organizations as legitimate development and diplomacy actors, not as curiosities.

Third, let's leverage the diaspora in trade and innovation more systematically. We've seen how immigrant-led businesses boost exports and diversify markets, and we can build on that. To that end, the Trade Commissioner Service could integrate diaspora business networks into its strategies—making diaspora businesspeople official "trade envoys" or forming mentorship pairs between established diaspora executives abroad and Canadian SMEs seeking to enter those markets. Likewise, in science and education, why not create a "global Canadians network" linking our researchers and alumni worldwide with projects here? Other countries aggressively court their scientific diasporas to collaborate and even return; Canada should do the same, especially given our need to stay competitive in R&D.

Fourth, and perhaps most importantly, culturally, we must celebrate the diaspora story as a core part of Canadian identity.

No more treating immigrants as outsiders after one generation or expats as people who left. We need to update our national narrative. Being Canadian can mean living in Toronto *or* London or Mumbai and still contributing to Canada's success. Likewise, being a proud Canadian can mean your parents came from elsewhere and you carry multiple identities. Embracing this plural, dynamic identity will help Canada navigate a future where diversity and global connectivity are the norm everywhere.

Canada's future will be shaped as much by those who venture out as by those who stay and as much by those who come here from abroad as by those born here. Our diasporas are Canada. They are just dispersed and circulating. It's time to bring them from the periphery to the centre of our vision for the country.

Canada's future will be shaped as much by those who venture out as by those who stay and as much by those who come here from abroad as by those born here.

We often talk about Canada punching above its weight on the world stage. The truth is, our weight class includes all our people, wherever they are. If we empower and partner with them, there's little we can't achieve. So let us move forward—boldly, unapologetically, and impolitely—in making diaspora engagement a cornerstone of Canadian strength. It's time to turn that untapped resource into an unstoppable force and turn our diasporas from footnotes into the frontline agents of change for Canada's next chapter.

Top (L): *A rare image of my strong-willed maternal great-great-grandmother, "Anaikoddai" Sinnamma Ramalingam (nee Kanthapillai), whose stories were passed down as legends within the family, including one of her impolitely taking on the local British magistrate during a legal proceeding. (Jaffna, early 1900s)*

Top (R): *My maternal grandparents who helped raise me, Rasiah Selvarajah and Sivayogam Subramaniam, shortly after they married. (Jaffna, 1948)*

Bottom (L): *With my parents, Sinnathamby Nadesalingam and Anusuya Selvarajah, on my first birthday. (Jaffna, 1982)*

Bottom (R): *With my mother after a school performance, unaware that I was going to be soon uprooted from Sri Lanka. (Jaffna, 1986)*

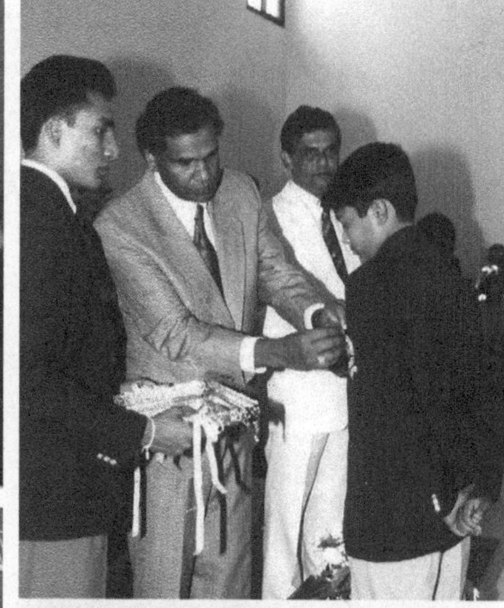

Top (L): *With my mother and siblings registering as refugees in India. (Chennai, 1987)*

Top (R): *First being called to serve—as a senior prefect in high school—not realizing that only a few months later I would be leaving Oman. (Muscat, 1997)*

ottom (L): *Taken on a recent drive down memory lane to the Tuxedo Court apartment complex where I lived in the te 1990s upon arriving in Canada. (Scarborough, 2025)*

ottom (R): *During a temporary ceasefire in the civil war, I returned to the traditional Tamil homelands in Sri Lanka r the first time since leaving as a child—this time to assist with grassroots capacity building efforts. (Kilinochchi, 2003)*

Top (L): *Taken in my early years as a civil servant when a three-month stint ended up becoming a fifteen-year career the Ontario Public Service. (Toronto, 2008)*

Top (R): *Observing Siklet or Ethiopian Orthodox Good Friday at Betä Giyorgis. (Lalibela, 2014)*

Bottom (L): *Paying tribute at the mausoleum of the poet Kahlil Gibran, a unifying icon for Lebanese Canadians w built a park in his honour in Edmonton, Alberta. (Bsharri, 2014)*

op (L): *Visiting the infamous Hôtel des Mille Collines during Kwibuka 20, which was a key backdrop for Lt. Gen. ₹et'd) Hon. Roméo Dallaire's harrowing account of his command of the United Nations peacekeeping mission in Rwanda uring the genocide. (Kigali, 2014)*

ottom (L): *Visiting Al-Maghtas or Bethany Beyond the Jordan, on the east bank of the Jordan River, which is venerated : the sacred site where Jesus was baptized by John the Baptist. (Balqa, 2014)*

ight: *Stopping by for a drink at the historical Strand Hotel in Myanmar, which has reportedly hosted several literary gures through the years, including Orwell, Kipling, and Maugham to name a few. Later that summer, Canada opened : embassy amidst the growing communal violence that eventually culminated in the Rohingya genocide. (Yangon, 2014)*

Top (L): *Visiting Tahrir Square, the focal point of the 2011 Egyptian Revolution during the Arab Spring movement. was still heavily guarded by a tank company, this time ironically against pro-Morsi protesters. (Cairo, 2014)*

Top (R): *Under the omnipotent presence of Chairman Mao while visiting Tiananmen Square on my first trip to Chin and completely taken aback by the warmth of the people I met everywhere I went. (Beijing, 2014)*

Bottom (L): *Standing in the shadows of Angkor Wat, the largest religious structure and Hindu temple in the world, bu in the early twelfth century and influenced by the powerful Chola Tamil kingdom with which the Khmer empire had military alliance. (Siem Reap, 2014)*

Bottom (R): *One of the most important moments in my life—leading a group of current and alumni diaspora voluntee from comdu.it to a tiny strip of beach where the Tamil genocide in Sri Lanka reached its bloody climax in May 20 which is now commemorated in Canada as Tamil Genocide Remembrance Day. (Mullivaikkal, 2017)*

Top: *My mother blessing Tharshiga and me on our wedding day, with her trademark sense of humor captured on film. What we did not know then is that she would unexpectedly pass away a few months later. (Vaughan, 2017)*

Bottom: *With Canadian journalist and author Steve Paikin, bonding over our shared love for legendary Ontario politician, former Premier Bill Davis. A year after appearing on TVO The Agenda, I decided to leave the provincial public service and venture into business instead. (Toronto, 2019)*

REIMAGINING CANADA'S PLACE IN THE WORLD

"Geography has made us neighbours.
History has made us friends.
Economics has made us partners."

—JOHN F. KENNEDY (IN HIS ADDRESS BEFORE THE CANADIAN PARLIAMENT)

CHAPTER 7

SHIFTING GLOBAL POWER DYNAMICS

IT'S NO SECRET that Canada's global power dynamics are shifting. America's domestic divisions and bouts of isolationism have left allies jittery, and there is little reason to expect a return to the post–Cold War Pax Americana heyday, that era when the US could orchestrate global affairs, anytime soon.[103]

For Canada, this erosion of the old order is both unsettling and energizing. Unsettling because our security and prosperity have long depended on the stability of US hegemony and the multilateral institutions it championed. Energizing because, in a genuinely multipolar world, middle powers such as Canada have more room to maneuver if we are shrewd enough to seize the moment.

Here's the problem. When US leadership falters, Canada's reflex is to look across the Atlantic. But despite strong economic and historical ties, Europe has not positioned itself as a true strategic alternative to the US for Canada. One reason is bandwidth: Europe has been consumed with its own set of crises. These include Brexit, a resurgent

Russia, an energy crunch, and internal political fractures, leaving little capacity to deepen ties with Canada.[104]

Moreover, while Canada and Europe have a robust framework for trade and cooperation in areas such as climate and digital policy, these achievements haven't translated into a broader geopolitical alliance. Europe's strategic gaze often turns inward or toward its immediate neighbourhood.

The uncomfortable truth is that both the US and Europe are in relative decline on the world stage. A European think tank bluntly noted that the US and Europe are "on the same side of today's geopolitical dividing line: both are declining powers."[105] Europe's share of global GDP and population is shrinking, and its influence in the Global South is waning as rising powers such as China, India, and regional blocs gain clout.[106]

While many Canadians identify with Europe's values, we cannot pin our future on a continent whose strategic weight is not what it was in the twentieth century. Europe will remain a vital partner culturally, economically, and diplomatically, but it cannot single-handedly replace the geopolitical anchor that the US has been for us. This realization leads to an inescapable conclusion: Canada must diversify its partnerships and stand more on its own in navigating the emerging multipolar order.

The Indo-Pacific region is an obvious place to start, but even within our hemisphere, we have options. Latin America, for instance, offers growth markets and like-minded democracies with whom we could collaborate more. In Africa, where the number of consumers is rising and great power competition is playing out, Canada has historical goodwill we could rekindle. The main point is that diversifying partners is no longer just a long-term aspiration; it's a strategic imperative for Canada's resilience.

At the same time, let's be realistic: We will never replace the United States in our calculus. Geography and economics decree that the US will remain our primary partner for the foreseeable future. But we *can* recalibrate from outright dependence toward a more balanced portfolio of relationships.

Courting the Two Giants

If the West is no longer the only show in town, Canada must court relationships with the new power centres driving the multipolar world. Two nations stand out: India and China. Their sheer scale and trajectory make them impossible to ignore.

In 2023, India surpassed China as the world's most populous country. It has a booming economy now ranking fourth in the world, is on track to soon overtake Japan for third place, and is the fastest-growing major economy. A youthful demographic, a vibrant tech sector, and a strategic position in Asia all make India a potential powerhouse of the twenty-first century. As the president and CEO of the Canada-India Business Council, Victor Thomas, cautions, "India is ascending, while Canada is declining. If we wait until India is standing on the economic podium, we'll be at the back of the line."[107]

Thomas argues the urgency comes not just from India's rise but from what Canada risks by remaining passive: "If we can't position ourselves better to do that now," he warns, "we're missing a huge opportunity for actual basic investment, bilateral trade, and also of importance, a geo-security ally in that region."

As Thomas points out, "We [Canada and India] have natural complementary economies and should be drastically increasing our trade together."[108] We share democratic institutions and a Commonwealth heritage, and Canada is home to a 1.3 million-strong Indian diaspora bridging our countries. Trade between Canada and India, however, remains strikingly underdeveloped, with roughly C$10 billion in goods, compared to over C$100 billion with China.

India's huge market aligns with Canadian strengths. We can export food to feed India's 1.4 billion people, supply potash fertilizer, partner in tech and education, and import everything from pharmaceuticals to skilled talent. Yet, candidly, the Canada–India relationship is strained. Decades of mistrust, policy missteps, and lately, a serious diplomatic rift have hampered progress.

So here is the hard truth: Speaking hard truths about India—on human rights, democratic backsliding, or diasporic politics—comes with real costs. Unlike in the "Canada the Moral Powerhouse" era, we are now dealing with a self-confident major power that does not respond kindly to public lecturing from Western capitals.

India's government is hypersensitive to external criticism. Even global heavyweights tread carefully. Mark Carney, for instance, has chosen measured language rather than public confrontation—because ambitions in India require diplomacy, not grandstanding. This is not cowardice; it is recognition of geopolitical reality.

The task for Canada is to find a new tone—principled yet pragmatic, frank in private yet disciplined in public. Engagement must continue, but without the sanctimony that characterized some earlier eras of Canadian diplomacy.

Then there is China. If India is the rising "democratic superpower" of the future, China is the here-and-now superpower challenger. It is the world's second-largest economy (and by some measures, the largest in purchasing power). It's Canada's second-biggest single-country trading partner, a top consumer of our commodities, and a source of everything from affordable goods to international students in our universities. For Canadian businesses, China has meant profit; for our consumers, lower prices. Yet, China embodies the thorniest dilemma in our foreign policy.

The arbitrary detention of two Canadians (the "two Michaels") in apparent retaliation for our arrest of a Chinese tech executive brought relations to a nadir from 2018 to 2020. Allegations of Chinese interference in Canadian elections and espionage activities persist. Beijing's turn toward authoritarianism at home and assertiveness abroad clashes with Canada's values and security interests, and made it clear that naïve engagement is no longer an option. How do we engage a country that is at once an economic linchpin and a systemic rival to the Western way of life?

Canada's path lies in calibrated engagement with eyes wide open. Decoupling entirely from China is neither feasible nor wise, as it would devastate certain Canadian industries (imagine our farmers and lumber exporters losing the Chinese market overnight) and cut us off from a major engine of global growth. At the same time, business as usual is untenable.

I believe Thomas is right when he points out that "for thirty years, economics drove geopolitics." But as he continues, "That's flipped. Now geopolitics drives economics. If Canada can figure that out, we have a great opportunity to do phenomenal business." But if we cling to the old assumptions, we'll be sidelined.

This change demands discipline. Thomas says bluntly, "Canada can and should be playing a much bigger role—but it can't be assumed that it happens naturally anymore. It has to be much more proactive and, dare I say, strategic." Selective de-risking is the name of the game. This involves tightening investment screening, safeguarding critical infrastructure and intellectual property from Chinese state influence, and coordinating with allies on a common approach.

But decoupling does not mean not talking. In fact, dialogue is more important than ever to prevent misunderstandings from spiralling. We should seek deeper trade ties with other Asian economies to reduce our relative dependence on China, which is a key goal of Canada's new Indo-Pacific Strategy.

Expanding Our Horizons

Beyond India and China, we must broaden our view to other emerging players. Southeast Asia is a region of immense promise for Canada. The ten ASEAN nations collectively form the world's fifth-largest economy and are growing rapidly. They sit at the nexus of Indo-Pacific trade routes and are actively seeking to diversify their partnerships beyond just China and the US. Canada belatedly recognized this by launching formal free trade talks with ASEAN and introducing the Indo-Pacific Strategy that rightly highlights the region.

But talk alone won't get us there. As Thi Be Nguyen, a longtime participant in Canada–ASEAN relations, put it sharply, "There needs to be not just strategies and plans. There needs to be concrete action to connect Canada to the world. The Indo-Pacific Strategy is a very good start."[109] And Nguyen isn't alone in this assessment. Business leaders and regional experts have repeatedly stressed the need for Canada to move beyond announcements and begin deploying real resources—both diplomatic and commercial—to deepen our presence.

Nguyen points out that while Canada is nominally a G7 country, its influence has dimmed: "Canada is fairly lost globally ... the reputation that Canada used to have ten years ago is no longer there. Canada is seen as an afterthought." Her diagnosis is blunt but necessary. Our polite restraint has cost us in a world that now rewards strategic clarity and unapologetic presence. As she explains it, "We need to stop seeing ourselves as an island. We live in an interconnected world and cannot afford to stay provincial in our thinking."

Vietnam, Indonesia, and the Philippines are all examples of where Canada's multicultural makeup, educational ties, and economic complementarity could unlock powerful new relationships. Nguyen noted that Vietnam has been Canada's largest trading partner in Southeast Asia since 2015 and that under the Comprehensive and Progressive Agreement for Trans-Pacific Partnership (CPTPP), our trade has surged. With Vietnam's economy projected to keep growing at more than 6 per cent annually, it is exactly the kind of market Canada should prioritize. The same goes for other ASEAN states. By establishing a stronger foothold in Southeast Asia, Canada not only finds new customers for its goods and services but also gains a toehold in the broader Indo-Pacific strategic theatre where global power dynamics will play out.

Execution is the missing link. Whether through expanding support for Canadian SMEs in ASEAN markets, codeveloping infrastructure or digital solutions, or locking in a Canada–ASEAN free trade agreement, we must stop treating Southeast Asia as a side project. In Nguyen's words, "We cannot just be the country of maple syrup and beavers anymore. That's not who we are. We're diverse, we're bold, and we need to act like it."

Elsewhere, the Middle East and Africa present different but equally important opportunities. These are regions rich in resources and ambition, with young populations and expanding markets. Canada has value to offer—especially in education, infrastructure, clean energy, and governance—but we must approach these relationships with a lens of mutual benefit, not moral instruction or aid proselytization.

Nguyen urges us to embrace what she calls "positive nationalism." This is a bold, unapologetic pride in who we are, rooted not in nostalgia but in the diversity, openness, and competence that define modern Canada. That requires shedding the old archetypes. "If we really believe in our diversity," she says, "then let's go beyond hockey and the maple leaf. Let's build new symbols that actually reflect the country we've become and take that confidence to the world."

Billionaires and Battlefields Without Borders

Power is not only shifting among countries. It's also flowing outside the traditional state system. In this new era, nonstate actors and even individuals can influence global events as never before. Canada must understand this dynamic because sometimes our dealings with a corporation or a tech mogul might be as consequential as dealings with other governments.

One striking illustration is the saga of Elon Musk and Starlink in the Ukraine war. When Russia's invasion threatened Ukraine's communications, Musk's SpaceX provided Starlink satellite internet that became a lifeline for the Ukrainian military and government. Suddenly, a private billionaire held sway over a critical piece of a nation's defence and communication infrastructure. When Musk later refused a Ukrainian request to enable Starlink for a drone attack, effectively vetoing a military operation, it raised eyebrows worldwide.[110]

For Canada, which prides itself on rules and institutions, this rise of nonstate power is disconcerting. How do we, as a sovereign nation, protect our interests when a single corporation might control the flow of information to our citizens or a single wealthy individual might buy out platforms that shape our public sphere?

Part of the answer lies in regulation and alliances. We need robust frameworks, ideally aligned with like-minded countries, to ensure transparency and accountability from tech giants. Internationally, we should be advocating for norms around things such as satellite internet provision in conflicts and data privacy standards to prevent abuses of power by nonstate players.

At the same time, we can partner with some nonstate actors to advance our goals. Canada's cooperation with philanthropic foundations and NGOs in global health and development can amplify our impact. Billionaire philanthropists such as Bill Gates have poured resources into causes such as vaccine distribution and climate adaptation, and aligning with them can do more good than what our aid budget alone achieves.

Likewise, Canadian companies and innovators are nonstate actors of our own that project influence overseas. A Canadian mining firm in Africa or a Canadian AI startup expanding in Asia carries our flag in subtle ways; how they act can burnish or tarnish Canada's image. So, engaging our private sector in a kind of "Team Canada" approach to global ventures can extend our soft power (e.g., encouraging Canadian firms to uphold high environmental and labour standards abroad, turning them into ambassadors of our values quietly).

We're also seeing the power of grassroots or leaderless transnational social movements in global affairs. Youth climate activists, decentralized hacker collectives such as Anonymous, or even diasporic protest movements can shape the actions of states. Canada's own policies may increasingly be influenced by such movements. Being attuned to these currents and engaging with them is part of modern diplomacy.

Canada Must Step Up to Lead

Rather than shrink from this moment, Canada should step up to lead. Canada has long relied on multilateral institutions, such as the UN, NATO, the WTO, the G7, the Commonwealth, and La Francophonie, as force multipliers. In a world of giants, we found safety and influence in rules-based clubs. But now that things are shifting, we must adapt and find new ways to lead. But as power diffuses and those same alliances fracture, Canada must adapt. Leadership now requires clarity, courage, and a willingness to take principled positions even when they come with political risk.

The UN, for one, is at a low ebb of efficacy. Great power rivalry has paralyzed the Security Council on major crises. The General Assembly is increasingly divided into ideological and geopolitical blocs. The General Assembly is often divided between blocs. And as noted earlier, Canada's own high-profile loss in the 2020 Security Council race—our second in a decade despite the campaign being personally led by Prime Minister Trudeau—was a sobering reminder that nostalgic reputation cannot substitute for meaningful engagement.[111] "We're still at the G7 table," Thomas says, "but we're not a top seven economy anymore, and we have not been invited with our natural allies to AUKUS or the Quad."

"Canada is fairly lost globally," Nguyen soberly adds. "The reputation we had ten years ago is no longer there. We're seen as an afterthought." Tough as this news might be to digest, it can serve as a valuable wake-up call that virtue signalling alone wins no votes and that our influence in the UN stems from concrete contributions, not a nostalgic reputation. If we want to lead in the UN system, we must do the hard work of contributing meaningfully to peace operations, investing in development partnerships, and building coalitions on specific issues.

One of those issues is the Israeli–Palestinian conflict. Canada cannot credibly campaign for a Security Council seat—or claim to champion a rules-based international order—while avoiding a straightforward acknowledgement of Palestinian rights, human suffering, and the long-term unviability of the status quo. We cannot win a Security Council seat without speaking up on this file and without meaningfully re-engaging with Africa, where many states viewed Canada's recent diplomacy as inattentive or transactional.

The political calculus is unavoidable: Would taking a principled, balanced stance on Israel–Palestine cost us in Washington? Under the Trump administrations, the answer may well be yes. His openly transactional approach to trade places Canada in a uniquely vulnerable position; speaking up could carry real economic risk. But Zohran Mamdani's recent electoral success and the drop in his approval rating at the time of this writing as well as growing bipartisan fatigue with unconditional support for policies that undermine long-term peace prospects suggest that a future US administration may not punish Canada for adopting a more balanced, rights-based position. The caveat is clear: Timing matters. Until Trump is off the board and the US political climate stabilizes, Canada must calibrate carefully. But silence is not a strategy, and equivocation is not leadership.

Tough as this news might be to digest, it can serve as a valuable wake-up call that virtue signalling alone wins no votes and that our influence in the UN stems from concrete contributions, not a nostalgic reputation.

Trade institutions such as the WTO are also under strain, largely because of big power tussles. Canada, being a trading nation, needs a functional global trade system. We led the Ottawa Group, an interim initiative to patch the dispute mechanism with ad hoc arrangements among willing countries. Such creative diplomacy is Canada at its best. But long-term, we need to help broker a grand bargain to update WTO so that it can accommodate China and others fairly.

That's a tall order, but Canada can carve a mediator role here, leveraging our good offices with both Western and some developing countries. If the formal institutions remain paralyzed, we might see more plurilateral agreements such as CPTPP or minilateral groupings on issues. We should be at the forefront of those, as we have been with CPTPP, because it's better to help set the rules in smaller clubs than be left out altogether.

The multipolar reality is also testing the broader concept of a rules-based international order that Canada often invokes. It's clear that the concept means different things to different players. The Global South voices have grown louder, asking where their say is in rules set by a post–WWII, Western-centric system. Forums such as the G20, which include emerging powers, have become as important as the G7 for global decision-making.

We saw, for instance, how India's presidency of the G20 in 2023 brought developing world issues such as debt relief and digital public infrastructure to the fore. Canada must adjust its diplomacy to engage beyond the like-minded. Sometimes that means swallowing disagreements and working pragmatically with not-so-like-minded states on common problems (e.g., climate change with oil-producing states or health cooperation with states under sanctions). Our ability to bridge traditional and emerging powers by forming ad hoc coalitions will be crucial. Interestingly, Canada's diverse population could help in this bridging. We have entry points culturally in many societies, as noted, which our diplomats can use to create rapport.

We should also not underestimate regional organizations. In a multipolar world, regional blocs such as the African Union, ASEAN, Mercosur, and the Gulf Cooperation Council hold more sway. These are avenues to influence regional norms and tap into collective markets. It's worth continuing and deepening these ties, perhaps even positioning Canada as a supporter and partner to regional integration efforts.

Finally, credibility in multilateralism comes down to consistency and coherence. If Canada says it supports something, we need to back it up. One criticism after our UN Security Council bid loss was that our rhetoric (championing climate action, peacekeeping, etc.) wasn't matched by leadership in those fields at the time, whereas Ireland and Norway had more concrete track records to point to. It was a humbling reminder that *doing* something is viewed more favourably than *talking* about it.

As we go forward, picking a few international initiatives to truly lead on could restore some of that sheen. To this end, Canada could spearhead a global effort on regulating AI and convene experts, draft guiding principles, and rally countries to sign on. Or it could take the lead on reforming the World Health Organization's pandemic response framework. When others see Canada taking initiative—real initiative, not rhetorical initiative—and contributing resources, our standing rises, and paradoxically, that strengthens the very multilateral system we need.

Indigenous Communities Have the Answer

As Canada adjusts to a world where power is no longer concentrated in one or two capitals, we're being forced to shed old assumptions and relearn how to move through global uncertainty. But for some, this isn't new terrain. It's lived experience.

Indigenous communities across this land have long known what it means to adapt when the world around them changes. They have experienced the loss of dominance, the erosion of sovereignty, and the imposition of foreign systems. And yet, they have endured. More than endured, they have preserved and evolved ways of thinking that remain deeply relevant. Ways of thinking that can guide the rest of us through this similarly disorienting global moment.

What we now call a multipolar world is not chaos. It is complex. And complexity is something Indigenous peoples have navigated for generations. Not through conquest or central control but through an emphasis on balance, interdependence, and relational accountability.

John Ralston Saul gets to the heart of this in *A Fair Country* when he writes, "We are a people of Aboriginal inspiration organized around a concept of peace, fairness and good government."[112] This is not just a matter of heritage. It's a blueprint for how to lead today.

When traditional power structures falter, the Western instinct is often to respond with more structure, more enforcement, more noise. But Indigenous philosophies suggest another way. One that values humility over dominance, reciprocity over extraction, and long-term relationship over short-term gain.

Treaty-making, for example, has often been viewed by settler governments as legal paperwork, historical formality. But in many Indigenous nations, treaties are ongoing covenants. They are meant to evolve and reflect the state of relationship between people. They hold within them a profound insight that genuine partnerships are not transactional but continual. This logic could be revolutionary in international diplomacy, where static alliances no longer serve the complexity of today's world.

Or consider the deep-rooted understanding of land not as property but as relative. In Indigenous worldviews, land is not a resource to be managed but a relation to be honoured. In an age of climate crisis, this worldview is not just morally resonant. It is strategically urgent. If Canada wishes to lead on environmental governance, it cannot do so by ignoring those who have been stewarding ecosystems here since time immemorial.

And then there is the principle of thinking seven generations ahead. This approach stands in stark contrast to the short-termism that defines so much of international politics. For Canada, this mindset could become a signature advantage, especially as the world searches for leadership on issues such as AI, food security, and global health infrastructure.

But none of this potential means much if we continue to marginalize the people who hold these perspectives. Saul calls it our single greatest national failure—the inability to internalize the peoples of this land as the senior founding pillar of our civilization.[113] We treat Indigenous wisdom as an add-on, not a centrepiece. As something ceremonial, not strategic. And in doing so, we miss the opportunity to draw from one of our greatest national strengths.

If Canada wants to lead with moral clarity and earn credibility in the eyes of a skeptical world, it must begin by living its values at home. That means genuine inclusion of Indigenous voices in foreign policy and global strategy. Not as a gesture but as a principle. It means resourcing Indigenous-led initiatives that reach across borders in areas such as education, sustainability, cultural exchange, and human rights. And it means owning the fact that Canada's place in the world will be shaped by how seriously it takes the voices and visions of those who were here first.

There is a certain irony in all this. As the world grows more fractured, Canada is looking for new models to navigate the disorder. Meanwhile, those models already exist. They have been practised on this land for centuries by people who have endured waves of change, disruption, and threats to survival. People who learned how to move forward without needing to dominate. People who know what it means to lose power and yet still carry wisdom.

"Idealism is fine, but as it approaches reality, the costs become prohibitive."

—WILLIAM F. BUCKLEY JR. (POLITICAL COMMENTATOR AND NOVELIST)

CHAPTER 8

FROM SHARED VALUES TO SHARED INTERESTS

OVER THE LAST five years, I've been on several trade missions, as I look beyond Canada's borders to expand our businesses at 369 Global. On a 2024 Team Canada trade mission to Southeast Asia, I kept hearing a common refrain that went something like this: "Why does your government keep talking about feminism and inclusive trade outcomes? We just want to do business and make money."

In adapting to a multipolar world, Canada will need not just new *partners* but a new *mindset*. I mentioned earlier that, for far too long, our foreign policy has revolved around values-based diplomacy and the loud championing of liberal ideals. There is much to be proud of in that tradition. But as global power diffuses, the harsh reality is that a virtue-first approach is yielding diminishing returns.

Many emerging powers and developing nations are frankly tired of being lectured by the West. As one candid analysis noted, Canada spent years pursuing a "principled" foreign policy, trying to reshape the world in our image, and in the process stopped listening to what other nations actually wanted or considering what was in Canada's own best interest.[114] We attached social strings to aid and engagement, assuming our model was universally desired. Meanwhile, countries in Asia, Africa, and the Americas were looking for partners, not saviours. They were looking for investment and infrastructure, not sermons on human rights.

This approach played well at home, aligning with Canadians' self-image as a force for good. But it often fell flat abroad. As Victor Thomas pointedly stated, "You don't start a relationship by pointing out someone's worst faults—*especially* if you don't bring solutions or follow through."

This is the kind of realpolitik that middle powers such as Australia have deftly managed, as they uphold core principles but cut deals when necessary. Even our closest allies have adjusted. The European Union still espouses human rights and democracy, but it has also actively engaged with China and courts energy from the Gulf, pragmatically juggling values and interests. The United States, under various administrations, has alternated between crusading for democracy and shaking hands with autocrats when expedient.

Canada must also make its own adjustments. To achieve this, it's important to grasp some context and the current dynamic.

The Tradition of Shared Values in Canadian Policy

Canada's international brand has long been tied to benevolent values. We often project an image of the virtuous broker—the middle power that advocates for human rights, peacekeeping, and liberal norms. This tradition has its roots in the post–World War II era and the Pearsonian peacekeeping legacy.

In the decades since, whether Liberal or Conservative, Canadian governments frequently frame foreign engagements in terms of values. We prefer to say we partner with nations with whom we share democratic principles, the rule of law, and respect for diversity. Domestically, too, shared values are invoked as the glue holding together a vast country of differing regions and cultures. From multiculturalism as official policy to the Charter of Rights and Freedoms, Canadian identity is wrapped up in noble ideals.

However, elevating values to the forefront of policy can create blind spots. Amarnath Amarasingam, associate professor at Queen's University, observed that there is "a difference between values as guiding principles and values as preconditions for partnership. The latter can be a recipe for isolation."[115] In other words, it's one thing to let our values inform our goals, but making identical values a strict prerequisite for cooperation often isn't realistic.

It's one thing to let our values inform our goals, but making identical values a strict prerequisite for cooperation often isn't realistic.

During the Justin Trudeau government, this tension became apparent. Trudeau's branding of Canada's "feminist foreign policy" and emphasis on LGBTQ+ rights and gender equality abroad earned praise from human rights advocates. However, it also sometimes put Canada at odds with potential partners. This was evident when Canada sought a deeper trade relationship with China in the late 2010s. Ottawa's insistence on including progressive provisions on gender, labour, and the environment was met with puzzlement and resistance in Beijing. The Chinese side was interested in steel, soybeans, and technology transfers, not lectures on feminism. In 2018, a Canadian tweet urging the release of Saudi women's rights activists triggered a rupture in relations; Riyadh expelled Canada's ambassador, froze new trade deals, and pulled students out of Canadian universities, underscoring how public rights advocacy can clash with partner priorities.[116]

"When Canada tied trade deals to labour and environmental standards, it sometimes felt like we were more interested in preaching than trading,"[117] Muraly Srinarayanathas quipped. His critique highlights how a values-forward approach, however well-intentioned, can backfire if it comes across as moralizing. In the Chinese case, talks stalled, and Canadian firms arguably lost an opportunity in one of the world's biggest markets because our government wanted the agreement to reflect our social agenda as much as our economic needs.

What Canada framed as a simple values-driven statement sparked a full-blown diplomatic rift. The cost to Canadian interests was tangible with the loss of business deals and diminished influence in the Gulf region, illustrating the high price of a clash between our values and another country's pride.

Similarly, in multilateral settings such as the UN, Canadian delegations often champion LGBTQ+ inclusion or women's empowerment. However, as Amarasingam noted, "In global forums, Canada's moral stands often win applause, but do they win us influence? That's debatable." Countries in the Global South, while perhaps admiring Canada's idealism, may find us out of touch with their immediate challenges of poverty, security, or development.

When Values Collide with Interests Abroad

One of the clearest arenas where Canada's values-versus-interests dilemma plays out is international diplomacy. In recent years, relations between Ottawa and New Delhi have been tested by value-laden issues. Canada's vocal support for freedom of expression allowed large Sikh diaspora protests and even extremist sympathizers to operate on Canadian soil—activities India views as threats to its national unity. Meanwhile, India's Hindu nationalist turn under Prime Minister Modi has raised human rights concerns that some Canadians find troubling.

The result is mutual suspicion. Canada champions pluralism and religious freedom, while India expects respect for its sovereignty and security concerns. What one side sees as a value (the right to advocate for political causes), the other sees as an attack on its core interests. Consequently, promising areas of cooperation such as trade, technology, and education are undermined by a lack of trust.

China represents the quintessential test of interest-based pragmatism versus value-driven caution. Economically, the interest is clear. China is the world's second-largest economy and a huge market for resources and services. Despite this, Canadian public opinion and politics are increasingly wary of Beijing's authoritarian model and human rights abuses, from Hong Kong crackdowns to Uyghur repression.

Ottawa's ban of Huawei 5G equipment and criticisms of China's record exemplify values influencing policy. Beijing responded with economic coercion, including trade restrictions on Canadian canola and the high-profile detention of two Michaels in apparent retaliation for the Huawei CFO's arrest. Reflecting on the China quandary, Amarasingam noted, "It's naive to think we can export Canadian values everywhere. Sometimes we need to deal with unsavoury partners for a greater interest."

Beyond Saudi Arabia, Canada's relations with other Middle Eastern states illustrate a cautious recalibration. Canadian governments have often talked about promoting democracy and women's rights in the region. Yet countries such as Qatar, the UAE, and Egypt—none of which fully share Canadian liberal values—are important players for trade, energy, and security cooperation. Recently, Canada has pursued closer ties with the UAE, despite the country's politics differing significantly from our own. This suggests a recognition that shared interests can trump value gaps.

Amarnath Amarasingam summed it up well: "Sometimes, stressing shared values is just a diplomatic nicety. When push comes to shove, nations—Canada included—act on interests." Thankfully, this pragmatic view is starting to resonate in Ottawa. Even leaders who philosophically prefer the language of values are finding that without an interests-oriented strategy, Canada risks being left behind in a world where others are cutting deals and forming alliances with whomever can help them achieve their goals.

Shared Interests at Home

The values-versus-interests debate isn't confined to foreign policy; it echoes within Canada's domestic sphere as well. A country as large and diverse as Canada contains different regions, cultures, and urban and rural communities, each with its own priorities and values. In recent years, we've seen a widening rural–urban divide and tensions between provinces that sometimes mirror the same dynamics we face abroad. Here too, a focus on shared interests might offer a path to unity that imposing shared values cannot.

Consider Western Canada, particularly Alberta and Saskatchewan. These provinces often emphasize values of economic freedom, self-reliance, and a skepticism about big government—values that can clash with the more progressive, collectivist ethos of urban centres such as Toronto or Montreal. Debates over carbon taxes, oil pipelines, and resource development frequently descend into moralizing. One side paints the other as unethical. You're either a "climate destroyer" or a "job killer."

"At home, if Alberta and Quebec only focused on their value differences, nothing would get done. Instead, think about the economic interests they share, and that's how we move forward," Srinarayanathas said, highlighting the need to reframe the conversation.

He's right. Alberta and Quebec might seem to have opposing worldviews, but they do share interests. Both want prosperous futures for their people, robust job creation, and world-class infrastructure. In fact, Alberta's energy wealth has long underpinned equalization payments that support services in Quebec and elsewhere, a literal sharing of economic interest across regions. Likewise, Quebec's hydropower and Alberta's oil could be dual pillars of Canadian energy security if we choose to see them as complementary assets rather than value-laden symbols.

The rural–urban divide presents a similar puzzle. Rural communities prize tradition, often leaning more conservative on social values, while big cities tend to be more liberal and diverse. These differences in outlook can breed political resentment, as seen in the rise of prairie populism or the sense among some rural Canadians that "Toronto elites" don't respect their way of life. Scratch beneath the surface, though, and common interests emerge: Both rural and urban areas need investment in infrastructure, both suffer when the economy falters, and both want safe communities and good schools for their children. "Rural and urban Canadians might not see eye to eye on social issues, but they both want jobs and growth. Those are shared interests leaders should harness," Srinarayanathas added, drawing from his experience in cross-country business.

A practical example can be found in broadband internet expansion. Urban tech entrepreneurs and rural farmers alike benefit from better connectivity. It's a shared interest that can unite unlikely allies. Similarly, infrastructure projects such as transportation links or energy grids often cut across partisan and provincial lines because they serve broad economic needs.

By focusing on these shared interests, Canadian leaders could reduce the zero-sum nature of our internal debates. Instead of framing energy policy as environmentalists versus oil workers, we could identify investments in clean technology that create jobs and reduce emissions—appealing to both values-driven and interest-driven constituencies. The same principle applies to issues such as healthcare funding, education, and housing: Rather than moralizing about what the government should do based on ideology, focus on tangible outcomes that benefit all Canadians. In practice, this might mean more federal–provincial negotiating in terms of economic payoff and less finger wagging about who holds the moral high ground.

Why Values Still Matter

None of this is to say Canada should abandon its values or hush its human rights voice entirely. As Canada moves from a foreign policy rooted in shared values toward one more attuned to shared interests, it's crucial to recognize what might be lost along the way. Interests may get deals signed. But values can build the trust that sustains them.

There's no question that a solely values-based approach where human rights or democratic ideals are nonnegotiable prerequisites can feel impractical in a world of transactional geopolitics. That said, a strategy based only on mutual interests has its own blind spots. "If you're willing to put interest above values," Amarasingam noted, "you have to realize it's only your values that are going to be compromised. Authoritarian regimes such as India, China, and Iran are not compromising theirs. They're winning because they're doubling down."

That's a sobering reminder. In many places, values are *not* window dressing. They are the core of how nations understand themselves. And so, if Canada chooses to adopt a more interest-driven posture, we need to do so with our eyes wide open. Our principles, even if flexible in expression, must not be discarded wholesale.

In our closest and most stable alliances—whether with the US, Japan, or key European states—shared values have created a kind of diplomatic margin for error. Even when disagreements arise, there's still a baseline of mutual understanding built on democratic norms and social pluralism. That's the kind of trust that smooths conflict and fosters long-term cooperation. Strip that away, and international relationships become brittle. A purely transactional alliance offers little cushion when interests diverge.

Here is a tough and complex example. In 2023, then–Prime Minister Trudeau publicly accused India's government of involvement in the murder of a Sikh activist in Canada—a grave allegation that India vehemently denied. Retaliatory expulsions of diplomats followed, and negotiations on a trade pact were paused. Was this the right course of action? I would argue that Canada's response was too aggressive and unnecessarily damaged our relationship with India. In contrast, Amarasingam would say that Canada did not do enough to respond to this "hit squad."

It's not that simple. I agree with Amarasingam, who said, "Most countries try to strike a balance between working with countries economically for mutual benefit but, at the same time, using that benefit to push a human rights agenda." That's where Canada must live. Right in that tension-filled middle. It's not clean, and it's rarely satisfying. But if we get the balance right, we can walk a narrow path between naive idealism and cynical dealmaking.

Here's one way to think about it: Values define the boundaries of Canadian foreign policy. Interests determine direction, but values mark the lines we won't cross. A smart strategy aligns both without pretending they're interchangeable. When done well, this approach still lets us pursue trade and innovation with governments we might disagree with while making clear what lines we won't cross and why.

Interests determine direction, but values mark the lines we won't cross.

There's also the matter of domestic accountability. Canadians expect their country to stand for something. The passport that opens doors in places such as Lebanon or Syria, as Amarasingam mentioned, does so not just because of our neutrality but because of the perception that Canada is fair, peace oriented, and principled. That soft power matters. If we become known as a country that makes deals without a conscience, that capital erodes.

This is why the next generation of Canadian leadership must walk with nuance. They must learn to be dealmakers and bridge builders but also defenders of core principles. They'll need to explain clearly why we work with some regimes and not others. Why we tolerate imperfection but draw firm lines at atrocity. Why we might do business with India or China while still advocating loudly for political prisoners or diaspora safety. Without that clarity, the policy becomes hypocrisy, and voters rightly revolt.

Ultimately, the move from shared values to shared interests isn't an abandonment. It's a recalibration. It's about maturing our global posture while remembering what has made our global image resonate in the first place. The impolite Canadian isn't rash or reckless. It's just someone who's done being taken for granted. Someone who negotiates with clarity and deals with realism but doesn't forget their soul in the process.

If Canada can strike that balance—interest driven but values anchored—we may yet emerge not as a naive moralist or a cynical trader but as something rarer: a principled power in an unprincipled world.

Our values *are* part of our national interest, and in some cases, speaking out is the right course. But we need to pick our spots and balance our objectives. A more pragmatic foreign policy means being driven by tangible Canadian interests, such as economic, security, and reputational concerns, rather than by a need to advertise our virtues.

Six Steps to Shift from Values to Interests

So, how can future Canadian leaders in government, business, and civil society operationalize a shift toward shared interests without abandoning what makes Canada, Canada? Drawing on insights from my conversations and the examples I've shared, here are some concrete ways to practise interest-based diplomacy and partnership building:

1. **Identify overlapping objectives**: When approaching a country or a province, start by mapping where our needs intersect. For instance, if an African nation needs infrastructure and Canada has engineering firms needing contracts, that's an overlapping objective. Begin the dialogue there, rather than with abstract discussions of democratic values.

2. **Separate channels for values and deals**: Rather than conflating trade talks with human rights discussions, create parallel tracks. Canada can continue to support NGOs, international institutions, and quiet diplomacy that promote our values globally but keep those efforts somewhat separate from the negotiating table where business is done. This compartmentalization ensures that progress on, say, a technology partnership isn't derailed because of an unrelated disagreement over social policy.

3. **Leverage diaspora networks**: Canada's diverse diaspora communities are a unique asset that can facilitate interest-based partnerships. As Srinarayanathas notes, "Our diasporas can be a secret weapon in interest-based diplomacy. They have the language, the contacts, the cultural know-how to create win-win projects others might miss." We should empower them as bridge builders.

4. **Think outside the political norms**: Interest-based diplomacy need not be government led alone. We can foster more Team Canada trade missions that include business leaders, provincial representatives, and even city mayors, all hunting for areas of mutual interest with foreign counterparts. These

missions should be less about ribbon cutting and more about closing deals.

5. **Focus on what we want**: By consistently discussing what Canadians want and how to achieve it, rather than invoking abstract unity values, leaders might actually foster more genuine unity. The federal government could convene first ministers around specific growth initiatives where every province has something to gain, focusing the discussion on dollars and jobs instead of the usual constitutional or values fights.
6. **Learn the art of the win-win**: A truly interest-based approach means always seeking the win-win outcome. This is a scenario where both Canada and its partner walk away better-off. This sounds obvious but requires skill. "I've learned as an entrepreneur that partnerships thrive on mutual gain, even if you disagree on a lot else," Srinarayanathas told me. Applying that ethos, Canadian negotiators should be less shy about striking deals that deliver tangible wins to counterparties. Over time, delivering win-wins builds Canada's reputation as a reliable partner.

Embracing these practices would mark a significant shift in how Canada conducts itself. It calls for a mindset change from seeing ourselves primarily as the world's conscientious Boy Scout to seeing ourselves as a savvy player balancing multiple interests. This doesn't mean becoming unprincipled. It means being strategic about when and how to deploy principles. Future leaders and entrepreneurs, unburdened by some of the twentieth-century myths of Canada always being the nice guy, may find this a liberating approach. They can be polite and professional, yes, but also impolite when needed, unapologetically pursuing Canadian interests first.

Canada has a lot to offer the world. But we need to shift from telling others what we stand for to understanding what they are actually looking for from us. That shift from values to interests might just be the key to making Canada not just a well-meaning country but a truly indispensable one.

"Unity, if it means anything, must mean that we can disagree without being disunited."

—STEPHEN LEWIS (DIPLOMAT AND HUMANITARIAN)

CHAPTER 9

EMBRACING OUR IMPOLITE FUTURE TOGETHER

ULTIMATELY, IF CANADA is to shift toward a more impolite future, unity will be the key. In a world that's increasingly divided, volatile, and uncertain, Canada has the potential to harness diversity as a strength, geography as an opportunity, and shared purpose as a lasting influence. But we cannot do that by staying comfortable or cautious. We must choose a path that is bold, deliberate, and collective.

We need a Canada where collaboration across regions, sectors, and cultures becomes our default mode. Not out of politeness but out of a deep commitment to shared interests. A Canada where the West and East, North and South, Indigenous and settler, urban and rural voices all find purpose in building something bigger than themselves.

Imagine what it would mean for Canadians to stand shoulder to shoulder in pursuit of a common purpose. A renewed sense that we rise or fall together. That our innovation, security, diplomacy, economy, and environment are not isolated challenges but pieces of one larger, national project.

Impoliteness Can Lead to Unity

It's ironic that as we adopt a tougher, more impolite stance on the world stage, this shift could actually be the force that brings us together at home.

When a country rallies around a bold, outward-facing goal, such as strengthening its global position, it creates a shared mission that transcends the usual lines of division. Differences between regions or political camps don't magically disappear, but they get reshaped by the urgency of that shared pursuit. Instead of avoiding conflict in the name of being polite, we're invited to wrestle with the real issues and work through them together.

A clear example is the long-standing tension between Western provinces, such as Alberta and Saskatchewan, and the rest of Canada. For years, people in the West have felt sidelined by federal environmental policies they see as stifling, often crafted by what they call the Laurentian elite. At the same time, many in Ontario, Quebec, and British Columbia have felt those two Prairie provinces were turning a blind eye to climate concerns. The result has been frustration, some separatist talk, and a whole lot of polite disagreement with little progress.

But when something external jolts the system—such as an aggressive trade move from the United States—you start to see those divisions blur. In moments of real challenge, Canadians tend to come together. That's when we remember that we're on the same team. And in those moments, the impulse to be bold rather than just agreeable can actually become the thing that draws us closer.

In moments of real challenge, Canadians tend to come together. That's when we remember that we're on the same team.

The recent shift on energy infrastructure is a case in point. After witnessing the turmoil south of the border, "We've never been this united in the country," said one energy CEO, regarding the newfound consensus that Canada must build its own capacity and not rely solely on the US.[118] Suddenly, politicians from Ontario to Newfoundland and the territories are talking about west-to-east and west-to-Asia pipelines as national projects, whereas before it was a mostly Alberta crusade.[119]

This suggests that a stronger approach, in this case, saying, "We're going to get it done, even if not everyone agrees 100 per cent," can actually reduce regional estrangement by focusing on a common goal of greater prosperity and autonomy for Canada. When people see that inaction is more costly than compromise, they become more willing to bridge differences. An assertive federal stance on critical infrastructure, coupled with fair environmental and Indigenous consultation, could finally end the paralysis and show all provinces that confederation is capable of nation building again. That's a unifying narrative we badly need.

Similarly, an impolite future can help bridge generational and cultural divides. Young Canadians often express frustration that the country isn't doing enough on existential issues such as global justice. Older generations might prioritize economic stability or national security. A purposeful Canada can marry these aims.

This is how impoliteness in the sense of decisiveness builds unity. It delivers tangible results that people can take pride in, whether it's a new high-speed rail connecting regions or a Canadian-led peace initiative abroad that captures the world's attention. Success on the world stage also tends to lift national morale.

Impoliteness Can Lead to Healing

We should also acknowledge how embracing a bold vision could start to ease the often-fraught relations between Indigenous and non-Indigenous Canadians. A truly strong Canada must include and empower Indigenous communities, not as an afterthought but as central partners, especially in areas such as the Arctic sovereignty, resource development, and cultural diplomacy. By actively involving Indigenous leadership in shaping our future to achieve things such as codeveloping an Arctic strategy or managing UNESCO heritage sites together, we mend internal wounds while projecting unity externally.

Impoliteness in this context might mean confronting uncomfortable historical and present truths and making big concessions such as sharing revenues or autonomy to ensure Indigenous peoples benefit from and lead in Canada's success. That might unsettle some, but bold action is often initially uncomfortable.

In the long run, however, nothing could strengthen Canada more than finally reconciling with Indigenous communities and moving forward together. Imagine the power of an Indigenous Canadian ambassador addressing the UN about a new model of partnership or an Inuit general leading a NORAD Arctic unit. Those images would do more for national unity and pride than a thousand polite summit statements.

The bottom line is that national unity is not served by standing still. It is built through common endeavours and, yes, occasional fights followed by resolutions. If Canada commits to a grand vision, say, to be the world's most reliable, innovative, and principled nation, and backs it up with policies, then Canadians from Vancouver Island to Newfoundland can feel part of something larger than their provincial or local identities.

We saw glimmers of this during the COVID-19 crisis, when governments and citizens rallied in an emergency. We see it when Canadian athletes, scientists, or soldiers excel internationally. We need to harness that energy in our politics and policy. Being impolite, in essence, means caring enough to argue, to strive, and to overcome our differences for a greater goal. In doing so, we may find that our divides start to narrow and that the Canadian mosaic strengthens.

Unity Is Possible

Looking back, Canada's greatest achievements have come when we have chosen bold national projects that forced collaboration and unity around a common cause. The very birth of Canada in 1867 was an exercise in constructive impoliteness. Our founders disagreed bitterly on many points, but they hammered out a daring new federation rather than remain polite colonies vulnerable to American takeover.

A century later, in 1965, political rivals Lester B. Pearson (Liberal) and John Diefenbaker (Conservative) clashed over adopting a new flag, but ultimately, Parliament chose the bold maple leaf design that unified Canadians under a distinct symbol. Even the near breakup of the country in the 1995 Quebec referendum was averted by an impassioned all-hands effort. Tens of thousands of Canadians from English- and French-speaking regions descended on Montreal for the last-minute Unity Rally, literally pleading with Quebec to stay.

Leaders who normally opposed each other stood shoulder to shoulder on that stage, making heartfelt appeals for a common future.

The "no" side's narrow victory was won not by unobtrusive silence but by a raw, exuberant confrontation with the possibility of division and a collective decision to remain together. These moments prove that, when faced with existential choices, Canadians can set aside differences and act in unison.

Canada has already seen glimpses of how a direct, purpose-driven stance can bring together people who usually disagree. When the stakes are high, Canadians from all political stripes, regions, and backgrounds have shown they can close ranks. Recent history offers several examples of unlikely unity in pursuit of national interests.

EXAMPLE #1: UNITING IN TRADE NEGOTIATIONS

During the 2017 NAFTA renegotiation with a protectionist US administration, Ottawa formed a special advisory council that included former adversaries from across the spectrum. The Liberal government invited figures such as Rona Ambrose (a former Conservative leader) as well as Labour and Indigenous leaders onto Team Canada.[120] They all worked together, even if they had clashed in domestic politics, to present a united front defending Canadian jobs and industries. This nonpartisan team effort sent a powerful message that when Canada's economic future was on the line, partisan differences took a back seat to the national interest. The result was a stronger negotiating position and a deal that preserved key aspects of our economy.

EXAMPLE #2: UNITING EAST AND WEST

Long-standing regional rifts have also softened when bold action is called. A prime example is energy infrastructure. After years of pipeline projects stalled by infighting, attitudes shifted dramatically once it became clear Canada could no longer rely on an unpredictable US market.

In 2025, Ontario's Premier Doug Ford—a populist from the industrial centre—and Alberta's Premier Danielle Smith—a libertarian from the oil-rich west—signed agreements to jointly push new oil pipelines and trade corridors across many regions of Canada. As Ford argued, "The best way to protect Canadian workers from tariffs and economic uncertainty is to build the infrastructure that will get our resources to new markets."[121] He even warned that relying on a single aging pipeline through Michigan (Line 5) left Ontario's economy vulnerable if the US shut it down.[122]

Facing this external threat, provinces that rarely saw eye to eye found a common cause. Leaders from the east to west coasts, conservative and progressive alike, agreed that Canada must control its own energy destiny—a consensus unimaginable a few years prior. As Premier Smith put it, the provinces were "joining forces to get shovels in the ground," building projects that connect "Canadian energy and products to the world."[123] Breaking a two-decade drought in major pipeline construction took this kind of impolite resolve, and it is forging a new alliance between regions once at odds.

EXAMPLE #3: UNITING ON THE WORLD STAGE

Canada's firm stance in foreign crises has likewise drawn broad support across usual divides. When Russia launched its brutal war on Ukraine, every single member of Parliament, from every party, voted to condemn Russia's atrocities as a "genocide."[124] Such unanimous votes are rare, but on core principles of human rights and sovereignty, Canada spoke with one voice. The federal government, backed by the opposition, swiftly imposed sanctions and sent aid to Ukraine.

Provincial leaders of different parties all welcomed Ukrainian refugees with open arms. Even normally cautious voices agreed Canada had to be bold and unyielding in the face of tyranny. This consensus transcended partisanship and signalled to the world that Canada's values are nonnegotiable.

A Clear Purpose Is a Great Cure for Division

What do these examples teach us? First, that a bold national purpose is the best antidote to internal bickering. When Canadians focus on what we are trying to achieve together, the usual quarrels over how to get there become secondary.

A bold national purpose is the best antidote to internal bickering.

A clearly defined mission—whether it's working toward economic independence, defending democracy, or building critical infrastructure—creates its own momentum. It gives everyone a role to play. Alberta roughnecks and Quebec intellectuals don't seem to have much in common but put them on the same mission of securing Canada's future, and they become teammates. In a culture of unity through impoliteness, arguing over details isn't a sign of division; it's a sign that people care enough to hash things out and then move forward.

Second, these stories show that unity doesn't mean unanimity. Being unified is not about every Canadian mirroring the same opinion or identity. Rather, it's about forging an agreement on the big picture and being willing to compromise on lesser points for the greater good. It's telling that even individuals known for principled opposition have been willing to join forces when it counts.

Environmental activists and oil executives might never agree on carbon policy in normal times, but many from both camps now concur that Canadian liquefied natural gas exports to Europe, for example, could undermine Putin's war chest and aid global stability. Such an impolite stance has environmentalists and oil executives engaging in dialogue, where they once only traded barbs. Unity grows when each side sees movement from the other. The impolite future calls for more of these unlikely alliances, where former opponents find at least one slice of common ground to act upon.

Finally, these examples underline a crucial point: Our diversity itself can be a source of strength if channelled toward shared goals. Canada's regional, cultural, and ideological differences mean we often have a 360-degree view of any problem. An impolite culture would encourage frank contributions from all sides.

Our diversity itself can be a source of strength if channelled toward shared goals.

A team comprising only like-minded polite people may avoid hurt feelings, but it seldom sparks the creative tension needed to tackle big challenges. A team of impolite but purpose-aligned Canadians, on the other hand, could be unbeatable because they bring every perspective and aren't afraid of honest debate.

Building a Culture of Constructive Impoliteness

If unity through bold action is the goal, how do we cultivate a culture of impolite Canadians unafraid to work together and speak up? It starts with reframing what politeness means in our national discourse.

Too often, politeness in Canada has been synonymous with avoiding tough conversations, glossing over conflicts, and deferring bold plans because we don't want to offend anyone. In politics and nation building, reflexive politeness can become a crutch. It can lead to the paralysis we've seen on issues such as climate action, Indigenous reconciliation, and constitutional reform, where leaders tiptoe around disagreements and nothing gets done.

A culture of constructive impoliteness would flip that script. It would treat open debate and dissent as signs of a healthy citizenry, not rudeness. Canadians would learn to air differences vigorously in pursuit of solutions, rather than smiling and nodding while quietly seething. This cultural shift doesn't mean abandoning civility or respect. We need to accept that constructive impoliteness is not about personal insults or chaos but about intention and the refinement of ideas.

Leadership must play a key role in setting this tone. Canadian leaders in the impolite future must lead by example in showing that collaboration doesn't require consensus on everything. Consider how the leadership during recent crises set a tone of unity. At the height of the pandemic, the federal government and provinces formed ad hoc Pan Canadian team efforts to procure vaccines and coordinate responses.

At one point, opposition members of Parliament literally joined the governing ministers in daily briefings and committees to expedite emergency aid. Parliament passed pandemic relief bills in a matter of days with all-party agreement—an unheard-of pace. Those measures weren't perfect, and there were loud debates over details, but no one doubted that every politician's priority was helping Canadians through the crisis. The usual partisan theatre was, temporarily, cast aside.

Create More Team Canada Tables

The lesson for peacetime leaders is to actively create more Pan Canada tables on major issues before they escalate to crisis level. A prime minister serious about unity could convene a cross-party, cross-sector council on achieving net-zero emissions or charting a strategy for the Indo-Pacific region, much as was done for CUSMA and previous NAFTA negotiations. By bringing diverse players into the process early and giving them ownership of the outcome, leaders can create the urgency and buy-in that typically only external threats can produce.

Another way to foster this culture is by celebrating candour and courage when we see it. We should positively reinforce those who take risks for the greater good. When a provincial premier decides to support an unpopular national initiative because it's right for Canada, we should applaud that bravery (even if we dislike the premier's politics otherwise). When Indigenous communities partner with industry or government on projects that balance development and heritage, we should herald those as models for the future. In an impolite Canada, no one should be scorned as a traitor or sellout for compromising in the national interest. Rather, compromise in this case should be a badge of honour.

We must remember that our system of federalism and democracy runs on compromise. The very act of confederation was a grand compromise among very different founding provinces. Every successful federal policy, from universal healthcare to the flag adoption, came from fierce debate followed by a middle ground. Reclaiming that spirit is essential.

Education and media also have roles to play. Schools could do more to teach constructive debate skills and the value of viewpoint diversity so that the next generation doesn't equate patriotism with merely being nice but rather with being involved. Too often, especially in media, the focus is on clashes and scandals. We no longer engage in deep explorative debate such as the Socratic method. Instead, we live in echo chambers with limited dialogue along lines of division.

Imagine instead a nightly news segment dedicated to the "solution of the week," featuring a collaboration between, say, a climate activist and an oil sands engineer finding common ground on clean technology. These narratives build a sense of possibility. They reinforce that being impolite can be done with mutual respect and yield real results.

Embracing Our Impolite Future Together

Ultimately, embracing an impolite future is about embracing ownership of Canada's destiny. It means no longer deferring to others to solve our problems or soft-pedalling when decisive steps are needed. Unity is the secret sauce that makes such boldness possible.

A lone leader or a single region cannot carry Canada forward. It must be all of us, moving in the same direction, even as we argue about the route. As the old African proverb says: "If you want to go fast, go alone. If you want to go far, go together."

What's encouraging is that the raw material for this unity is already present. When push comes to shove, Canadians do rally and find consensus on big decisions. The challenge now is to harness that instinct proactively, not just reactively.

We shouldn't have to wait for another crisis or trade war to realize we share a common purpose. By choosing a clear direction and acting with impolite conviction to pursue it, we can create the momentum that pulls the nation together by default.

This future is within reach if we choose it. Unity and impoliteness may sound like an odd pairing, but in truth, they reinforce each other. An impolite future calls each of us to participate and not just observe. It calls us to voice disagreement when it matters but also to listen and find solutions, rather than retreating into regional or ideological corners. If we answer that call, we will develop a deeper unity, the kind forged not by shallow niceties but by weathering storms together and coming out stronger.

In a world growing more divided and volatile, Canada's unity can be our superpower, and our impolite boldness can be our engine. We can be a country that argues, innovates, challenges, and builds—and that stays unified through it all.

Top (L): *With my friend and business partner, Muraly Srinarayanathas, at the Rideau Club. (Ottawa, 2022)*

Top (R): *With the 369 Global team at our very first town hall. (Ajax, 2022)*

Bottom: *A* majlis *meeting with His Highness Sheikh Nahyan bin Mubarak Al Nahyan to conclude a private B2B tra mission that I helped lead to the United Arab Emirates. (Abu Dhabi, 2022)*

op (L): *With Sahana and Karthik at the birthplace of the Canadian Confederation. (Charlottetown, 2023)*

op (R): *On a whistlestop tour of India's massive innovation ecosystem, starting at the Jio Innovation Lab located within eliance Corporate Park. (Navi Mumbai, 2023)*

ottom: *Memorable meeting with J. Y. Pillay, the sole survivor of Lee Kuan Yew's "Eight Immortals," a group of pioneering vil servants who built Singapore. (Queenstown, 2024)*

Top (L): *At a cybersecurity training summit co-hosted by 369 Global and AfricaHackon. (Nairobi, 2024)*

Top (R): *One of the things I've cherished the most is the opportunity to have my children join me on some of my busin travels, thanks to the support from Tharshiga and my wonderful colleagues. (Ho Chi Minh City, 2024)*

Bottom (L): *Speaking at the Global Tamil Economic Summit in Switzerland. (Davos, 2024)*

Bottom (R): *Helping launch 3 Magazine in the United States with the cover star, futurist Sinead Bovell. (New Yo City, 2025)*

op (L): *Celebrating with graduates at one of our annual convocation ceremonies at Computek College—recognized as one ' Canada's top growing companies—which trains nearly 2,000 domestic adult learners every year for vocational careers healthcare, technology, and business. (Toronto, 2024)*

op (R): *Visiting my father in Oman as he was wrapping up four decades of his life living and working in the sultanate, hich began during the reign of its visionary former ruler, Sultan Qaboos bin Said Al Said. (Muscat, 2024)*

ottom: *Awarded as Inspirational Leader of the Year at the CanadianSME Magazine's National Business Awards. 'oronto, 2025)*

Top (L): *Sahana and Karthik at th first powwow to celebrate National Ina enous Peoples Day. (Midland, 2025)*

Top (R): *In recent years, I have come understand the importance of stepping o from behind the scenes to share my p spectives more publicly, such as on sor systemic issues facing paid and unpa caregivers at the National Caregivi Summit in this instance. (Ottawa, 202*

Bottom: *Our True North, strong and fr (Brampton, 2025)*

PART IV

THE WAY FORWARD

"Risk more than others think is safe. Care more than others think is wise. Dream more than others think is practical. Expect more than others think is possible."

—CLAUDE T. BISSELL (THE EIGHTH PRESIDENT OF THE UNIVERSITY OF TORONTO)

CHAPTER 10

ECONOMIC IMPERATIVES IN A COMPETITIVE LANDSCAPE

CANADA IS NOT short on assets. We have talent, resources, stability, and a global reputation for openness and inclusion. But in an increasingly cutthroat world, potential is not enough. The global economy is shifting fast. If Canada wants to remain relevant, we must stop admiring our ingredients and start cooking with intent.

Competitiveness today is about reducing friction. Every unnecessary barrier, every month lost in bureaucracy, every opportunity slowed by outdated rules has a cost. And while we might pride ourselves on civility, the modern economy does not wait for polite consensus. Other nations are moving aggressively, rolling out red carpets for talent, cutting red tape for business, and building partnerships at warp speed. Canada must match that energy or fall behind.

We are at a crossroads where leadership will be measured not by how well we manage the status quo but by how decisively we reinvent it. This is a moment to act with precision, to redesign the machinery of our economy so that it actually serves the people and ideas it's meant to empower. It's about being bold enough to fix what's broken, even when that means rethinking deeply embedded systems, institutions, and habits.

The stakes are clear. We can either shape the next chapter of our economy with purpose or let it be written for us by others with sharper elbows and faster reflexes. Canada has everything to gain—but only if we are willing to *compete*, not just *participate*. Here are six imperatives we must embrace.

We are at a crossroads where leadership will be measured not by how well we manage the status quo but by how decisively we reinvent it.

Imperative #1: We Must Remove Internal Trade Barriers and Boost Labour Mobility

Historically, one of Canada's paradoxes is that, while we tout one economy, our provinces often operate like different countries. Crossing from British Columbia to Ontario can be as jarring to skilled workers as moving between Canada and the United States. As Shamira Madhany, the managing director and deputy executive director at World Education Services (WES), points out, we must radically reimagine the Canadian Free Trade Agreement. The original pact was about goods and services; we "forgot the people part."[125]

Madhany argues for a wartime-effort pace to reform, with an aggressive deadline to eliminate provincial licensing and regulatory hurdles. Thankfully, there is reason for optimism. In the throne speech to reopen Parliament following the spring 2025 federal elections, King Charles read Prime Minister Mark Carney's mandate of "building one Canadian economy by removing barriers to interprovincial trade."[126] As King Charles noted,

> By removing these barriers that have held back our economy, we will unleash a new era of growth that will ensure we don't just survive ongoing trade wars, but emerge from them stronger than ever. It will enable Canada to become the world's leading energy superpower in both clean and conventional energy. To build an industrial strategy that will make Canada more globally competitive, while fighting climate change. To build hundreds of thousands of good careers in the skilled trades. And to build Canada into the world's leading hub for science and innovation.[127]

Prime Minister Carney's mandate makes clear that Canada must connect and transform our country with nation-building projects, not just splinter it. In practice, this means engineering a seamless labour market. After all, why shouldn't a physician licensed in Winnipeg immediately treat patients in Halifax?

Madhany highlights the delicate line that licensing organizations such as the Ontario Medical Association must walk: "Although licensing bodies for doctors, nurses, and engineers need to uphold Canadian standards, they must balance that with transparent and objective assessment criteria," she says. Furthermore, provinces need to move toward working together collaboratively rather than bilaterally so that we can focus on Canada's, and not just each province's, competitiveness. The imperative is that domestic internal trade needs to enable the movement of resources, including people and talent, across the country with much less friction.

Real reform would be radical. Provincial colleges could mutually recognize credentials or even cede some powers to a federal council for key trades and professions. We've seen sparks of this idea in Ontario's recent "patchwork permit" for professionals. This raises an interesting question about what would happen if Ottawa took on licensing for a profession entirely, rendering obsolete the long queues at each provincial board.

These ideas sound audacious, but consider that provinces fought free trade with each other well into the twenty-first century. Reducing barriers would turbocharge job matching, reduce resentment, and give companies a single national market. One thing that all sides, from business to unions, agree on is this: *One market means more opportunity*. As the mandate letter warns, our "weak productivity" and regional fragmentation strain the economy.[128] Fixing internal trade will be foundational for the growth we need.

Imperative #2: We Must Attract Rather Than Subtract Talent

If talent is the new oil, Canada is an undertapped super tank, ready to import and refine the best of the world's brains. In the throne speech, the government urged Canada to "attract the best talent in the world to build our economy," even as it sets caps on temporary foreign workers and international students.[129]

In effect, Ottawa is telling global professionals and entrepreneurs this: "Canada is open for business. Come build here, and tell your friends." This message is no luxury. In today's fierce international talent chase, countries such as the US, the UK, and Germany have rolled out red carpets for innovators and skilled migrants.[130] Canada cannot afford to gawk from the sidelines.

Thankfully, we're seeing some forward progress. The vice president of Canoe Financial, Rohan Thiru, notes that young immigrants now routinely return to Canada.[131] Many doctors and engineers who fled south for higher-paying jobs in the US are now realizing that Canada is a safer and more stable option. While I've noted the historically large brain drain, there are signs of a brain gain.

Thiru laughs that *he* used to counsel clients to invest in Canada. Now, savvy entrepreneurs are reaching out to him. But they will only come if we make it easy. This means both expanding visas and easing settlement. Golden visa schemes (like some European countries offer for investors) might not be the best option, but we do have programs such as the Start-up Visa and provincial nominee streams.

We need to turbocharge this process and tangible incentives. Canada's postsecondary institutions should market themselves harder and in different regions of the world. Over a million international students enrolled in 2023, contributing nearly $31 billion to our GDP.[132] Yet clear housing issues have put this in tension.

The broader point is that Canada must consciously brand itself to talent. A recent analysis by the Montreal-based Institute for Research on Public Policy warns that as perceptions shift (housing crunch, political noise), we risk slipping in attractiveness.[133] But our multiculturalism and inclusive ethos are powerful magnets. As already stated, we must leverage diaspora networks—the overseas communities of Chinese Canadians, Indo-Canadians, and many more—as bridges for trade and ideas.

The *State of Trade 2023* report finds that immigrant entrepreneurs export to more diverse markets than Canadian-born peers.[134] In practice, this means a Montreal-based dispatch company owned by a Korean Canadian might ship to Asia as quickly as it does to Europe. We should strengthen networks such as Global Affairs Canada's Trade Commissioner Service in key diaspora hubs.

At home, we must dismantle "unearned obstacles" for skilled newcomers. Thiru points out the absurdity that we bring in qualified doctors or engineers and then make them start at the bottom rungs. "How do we employ them immediately instead of making them drive Uber for the next ten years?" he asks. This is a human capital crisis. We funnel immigrants into menial jobs because licensing lags behind.

Addressing credential recognition (as WES has championed) would unleash prodigiously trained professionals. In short, boosting immigration alone is not enough. Integration is key. We need apprenticeship blitzes, fast-track exam intakes, and incentives to hire immigrant-owned businesses. If the government wants to "build a Canada worthy of our children and grandchildren," as Carney pledges,[135] it must make use of every educated resident already here.

Imperative #3: We Must Lead the Way in Innovation

Canada has a storied history of punching above its weight in research, from the discovery of insulin to pioneering neural networks. Yet, too often, our intellect has been exported overseas or stymied by risk-averse capital. Thiru is blunt, stating, "We were the innovators in AI … and unfortunately, we didn't have enough capital to monetize on that." He points out that Canada's universities churn out top-tier STEM graduates, but startups inevitably decamp south, chasing dollars. The cure is twofold: Unleash domestic R&D investment and regulate smartly.

Across the country, companies are developing breakthroughs in cleantech, biotech, fintech, and more. The federal government explicitly recognized this in its mandate, noting that we must harness the "transformative nature of AI" to create opportunities across sectors.[136] That means not fearing automation but using it to build faster. Imagine AI-driven construction robots that can assemble affordable homes overnight or generative design algorithms accelerating chip development.

Canada should build on the Pan-Canadian Artificial Intelligence Strategy, which was recently announced by the federal government. Madhany notes that deploying AI and other leading-edge technologies at scale, by turning research into real projects, will be a core economic imperative.

Policy will be crucial. We need a mission-driven approach, such as government R&D grants aligned with national goals, stronger tax credits for next-gen ventures, and perhaps a sovereign innovation fund to seed deep tech firms. Thiru suggests concrete steps such as loosening capital requirements on banks so more loans flow to startups, slashing corporate tax rates for R&D, and even creating a Canada growth fund for science. Beyond money, we must signal welcoming arms to global talent in tech hubs. Startup visas with hefty innovation criteria should be matched with streamlined permanent residency.

Leadership in AI regulation also matters. If Canada can frame ethical guardrails of privacy, safety, and competition early, it can shape global norms and give local firms an edge, rather than forcing them to scramble to catch up. Prime Minister Carney has himself championed building tech into the centre of strategy, even appointing a dedicated AI minister in his government.

We must marry that ambition with on-the-ground initiatives, such as more superclusters, expanded incubators in smaller cities, and public sector adoption of AI to prove value. The mandate letter envisions the government "deploying AI at scale, by focusing on results over spending."[137] If bureaucracies can use AI to speed up permits or social benefits, citizens will see its benefits firsthand, and tech companies will have the government as the first client.

Imperative #4: We Must Have an Ethical Energy Diplomacy

Canada's vast resources of oil, gas, and minerals have always been a double-edged sword. We must exploit them, yes, but wisely and ethically, to reshape our role in the world. The throne speech and recent analyses speak of Canada as an "energy superpower," breaking US dependence and forging new alliances.[138] In practice, this means reversing years of pipeline paralysis and marketing our clean(er) hydrocarbons to friendly countries.

It also means leadership in natural resource diplomacy. We have an opportunity to unlock our energy potential, even if it means putting the pipeline debate to rest in Canada and actively exporting what we have, from liquified natural gas to potash, a mineral fertilizer in global demand. If there is a pipeline deal, it will need to be one that involves Indigenous partnership and equity to enable corridors from Alberta to tidewater.

In fact, this is already happening. In 2024, the Alberta Indigenous Opportunities Corporation announced an unprecedented equity purchase by First Nations in TC Energy's giant gas pipeline network.[139] It will allow dozens of Indigenous communities to own a stake in that infrastructure, "leading the world with [an] innovative approach" to Indigenous equity, as TC Energy put it.[140] These joint ventures show how resource projects can be both profitable and just.

Canada's new energy minister, Tim Hodgson, a former private sector executive, appears intent on a pragmatic pivot. The language of the mandate ("become an energy superpower") suggests massive scaling of both conventional and clean projects.[141] But we must strike a balance between climate goals and economic opportunity. One advantage is that our oil and gas are among those with the lowest carbon intensity in the world. If they are transported via pipelines efficiently, we can position them as transitional fuels for Europe and Asia, a geopolitical win.

Domestically, this vision has ties to reconciliation and infrastructure. Madhany highlights how the throne speech doubles a loan guarantee fund (to $10 billion) specifically for Indigenous ownership of major projects.[142] This reveals a government push toward Indigenous-led infrastructure corridors. When citizens of Fort McKay or Alexis Nakota Sioux Nation in Alberta can invest in pipelines, the social licence hurdle drops, and economic gains spread more fairly.

We also must diversify beyond oil. Canada has vast wind, solar, and hydro resources, and selling climate-friendly energy or minerals such as nickel can align profit with purpose. Just as Europe is bending to dependence on Russian gas, Canada can offer security of supply to NATO allies. Our tech, for example, a carbon capture or small modular reactor, could be our next export. The Trudeau era's hesitation on pipelines damaged global trust; the new government must repair it with credible deals.

Finally, energy diplomacy will mean balancing climate and business. Carney's government talks a big game on fighting climate change[143] while also pushing industry. This tension must be managed with nuance. Canada can become the one country that responsibly ports oil *and* leads on carbon pricing and green tech. To do this, it will need to stand firm on free trade (as Carney notes, the global trading system is in flux)[144] and negotiate from strength with allies.

Imperative #5: We Must Have Immigrant-Led SMEs and Global Diaspora Networks

Behind every pipeline and startup, there are entrepreneurs, many of them immigrants. Across Canada, SME owners from South Asian, African, Caribbean, and other communities are quietly powering trade. The *State of Trade 2023* data reveal the important truth that immigrant-founded small businesses tend to export to *more* countries than others.[145] Our diaspora literally carries our flag into new markets, using family ties and cultural fluency to bridge Canada with Asia, Africa, and beyond.

To leverage this, the government must amplify support for immigrant-led SMEs. Trade commissioner offices already have women- and Indigenous-led programs, so why not a diaspora partnership initiative? Imagine a trade mission where Indian Canadian business leaders connect Canadian tech firms with Mumbai, or a Chinese Canadian SME helping Canadian farmers export to Shanghai.

These networks already exist informally, and formal recognition and matchmaking could multiply their effect. As the *State of Trade 2023* report suggests, inclusive trade strategies from e-commerce grants to translation services help underrepresented exporters.[146] We should direct those strategies at diaspora communities.

Domestic measures include easing the path for foreign entrepreneurs to run businesses here. Startup visas should link with incubators run by diaspora entrepreneurs. We can also invite members of our diaspora to be Canada's first ambassadors in key global innovation events. The government might even consider an annual forum of global Canadian innovators, mirroring Ireland's diaspora networks. This taps into the simple truth that many newcomers came from world-class ecosystems, and their global mindsets benefit us all.

Immigrant-owned SMEs also create jobs locally. As Thiru notes, we should empower "foreign money" to flow into startups rather than overheated real estate. Targeted tax incentives or matching grants could redirect investment. Some provinces have experimented with venture capital funds focused on tech, and federal matching or loan guarantees can de-risk that. The goal is to spare our college grads (such as Thiru's sons) from brain drain and instead have overseas capital building unicorns here.

It's worth repeating that diaspora networks and immigrant businesses are the underutilized heroes in Canada's economic tale. Recognizing them isn't just good equity—it's smart economics. If we give these entrepreneurs the tools of better credit, mentorship, and trade missions, we multiply their contributions. It's the essence of an inclusive economy that "works for everyone," as Carney promised.[147]

Imperative #6: We Must Form Indigenous Partnerships in Infrastructure and Innovation

No review of Canada's economic future can ignore Indigenous peoples, who represent an essential partnership yet to be fully embraced. Madhany highlights the Carney government's commitment to Indigenous-led nation building. Doubling that $10 billion loan program makes Canada the world leader in funding Indigenous equity in projects, a policy long championed by groups such as the Canadian Council for Indigenous Business.

This translates to real projects, and we can already see it in energy. The TC Energy pipeline deal,[148] partly underwritten by that fund, allows nearly one hundred First Nations to share ownership of a major gas grid. Similar models could apply to green corridors—think hydro lines or EV charging networks run by consortiums of tribal councils.

Madhany hints at an "Indigenous-led energy corridor," which could connect Alberta's fields to markets in British Columbia and the northern US. Such infrastructure would not just carry electrons or gas, but it would also carry reconciliation forward. Profits flow to communities, and ownership means stakeholders are buyers, not blockers.

Beyond energy, Indigenous partnerships extend to tech and knowledge. The government's mention of a Canadian digital partnership with Indigenous communities indicates new pilot projects, which could create fibre networks or data centres in the North, where Indigenous knowledge guides development. If done right, this could empower remote communities with jobs and connectivity, making them partners in nation building, not afterthoughts.

All this aligns with the new spirit of Canada's mission of innovation and development achieved by true nation-to-nation collaboration. It's not just morally right—it's smart growth. When local knowledge holders help design projects, we avoid costly conflicts and cultivate a wider base of talent and ideas. In practice, that means making sure the excitement surrounding AI and the dollars of pipelines also reach Cree, Innuit, and Innu alike. In these ways, Indigenous partnerships can turn Canada's economy from a single track into many interwoven threads, stronger and more resilient for it.

Canada's Competitive Future

Putting all the pieces of trade, talent, technology, resources, and partnerships together paints a picture of what success could look like. Economic prosperity in Canada would mean airports and train stations humming with people moving freely for work, from coast to coast to coast. It would mean tech startups in Edmonton getting funding as readily as condo speculation in Toronto. It would mean an immigrant scientist in Vancouver inventing a breakthrough and finding VC backing without leaving the country.

Madhany and Thiru both express cautious optimism. As Thiru put it, he believes "Canada is going to be the place to be in terms of innovation, in terms of how well the economy is going to do" so long as we don't "fall asleep at the wheel." The path forward is clear: We need to vigorously remove old barriers, actively attract skilled people, vigorously invest in science and AI, market our resources ethically, and lift up those at the margins.

This bold agenda, rooted in hard-nosed policy and the stories of people on the ground, reflects the emerging impolite Canadian ethos. We will no longer meekly beg for crumbs on the global stage but confidently claim our share by unleashing every advantage we have.

Canada's challenges—from housing prices to climate change—are real, but we have the equally real advantages of diversity, stability, and determination. By aligning them with fresh policy vigour, we *can* achieve the "largest transformation of its economy since the Second World War" envisioned in the throne speech.[149] That transformation will look like a Canada where an engineer from Waterloo literally powers a farm in Africa with homegrown solar tech, where a doctor from the Philippines is saving lives in Ontario within weeks of arrival, and where a small-town pipeline worker can see their county benefit tangibly from resource wealth.

In the end, the economic imperatives are simple in concept but profound in action. We need to break down silos, unleash talent, innovate relentlessly, and build partnerships across all divides. As Prime Minister Carney reminds us in his mandate, Canadians will hold their government to the promise of real cabinet teamwork with provinces, Indigenous peoples, and industry.[150]

We need to break down silos, unleash talent, innovate relentlessly, and build partnerships across all divides.

This is not just a technocratic agenda but a renewal of the Canadian promise itself. If we succeed, the next chapters of our national story, and this book, will be written not just in polite compromise but in bold conviction that Canada can still defy the odds and lead the world by example.

"If you're not a little bit uncomfortable, you're not doing it right."

—RYAN REYNOLDS (ACTOR, ENTREPRENEUR)

CHAPTER 11

FOSTERING A CULTURE OF AMBITION AND INNOVATION

THE CHALLENGE OF living in a great country like Canada is that we often take many of our blessings for granted. As Goldy Hyder, head of the Business Council of Canada, wryly observes, too many Canadians act as if "we were born on third base and think we hit a triple."[151] We coast on inherited advantages and assume success will come easily. And little by little, this third-base mentality leads to complacency.

Many Canadians seem content to settle into a comfortable, average way of life. Talent and hard work can get muted in a culture that values politeness and predictability over hustle.

Hyder illustrates this with a simple retail anecdote. Walk into a store in Toronto at 8:50 p.m., and the clerk's first words are, "We close in ten minutes." Try that in Mumbai or Bangalore, and you'll find a very different attitude, as the shopkeeper would stay open all night to make a sale. "Here, that culture of 'good enough' has captured a lot of us," Hyder notes.

He sees a deep aversion to standing out or winning. "Everybody should get a participant ribbon; how dare you try to win a medal?" he chuckles, quoting the old refrain. In other words, Canadian society can seem to resent those who break the mould, and we too often demand "the great average" instead of celebrating excellence.

This mediocre mindset is dangerous for innovation. By hesitating to be excellent, Canadians risk being leapfrogged by more ambitious societies. In Hyder's words, we deserve better role models: "We should do in the economy what we do in sports ... aspiring to be great, to win at the things we can do."

By hesitating to be excellent, Canadians risk being leapfrogged by more ambitious societies.

The 2010 Vancouver Olympics were a perfect illustration. When Ottawa invested resources in its top athletes, Canada rose to become the top nation in the Winter Games. And I believe that if we treated our economy with the same zeal by investing in our strongest companies and industries, we could achieve a new kind of podium finish.

AtkinsRéalis, formerly known as SNC-Lavalin, offers another lens on Canada's culture of ambition. Headquartered in Montreal, the company grew into one of the world's largest engineering and project management firms, managing billions of dollars' worth of projects across continents. Unlike many Canadian firms that downplay their origins, AtkinsRéalis never hesitated to fly the maple leaf abroad, proving that global scale and Canadian identity can coexist.

However, the firm's legacy is overshadowed by scandal. Corruption and bribery allegations, culminating in criminal charges, shook public confidence in the company. What's revealing is how few Canadians came to its defence. For all its global reach, AtkinsRéalis had little reservoir of goodwill at home. Canadians seemed almost relieved to let the company bear the consequences of its misconduct, a stark contrast to the way Americans often rally around their corporate champions.

The lesson is sobering. Ambition alone is not enough. It must be coupled with integrity and public trust. AtkinsRéalis showed that Canadian companies can build global empires, but it also highlighted how fragile those empires become when the cultural reflex is suspicion rather than pride. For Canada to cultivate more global champions, we must learn to pair ambition with values, ensuring that success is celebrated not just abroad but also at home.

Abdullah Snobar, executive director of DMZ, world's largest university-based business incubator, warns that polite modesty can hold us back. He points out that Canadian startups often lose out simply by being "too polite about pushing out the message."[152] "Canada has developed some of the best innovations on the planet," Snobar says, but "we're too polite about having the humble brag." We underplay our wins. In contrast, he argues, now is the time to become confident promoters of Canadian talent.

If we want a culture of ambition, leaders must break the mould of caution. Politicians and executives alike need to reward risk and excellence, rather than defaulting to the lowest common denominator.

Seizing the Moment

Recent years have made clear that Canada's comfort can be a liability. But this crisis of confidence can be a catalyst for change, if we seize it.

As Hyder warns, "This is the moment of existential choice." If Canada returns to its usual routine once the crisis passes, we'll squander the urgency.

"I worry we will go back to regularly scheduled programming and say, 'I'm still on third base,'" he says. But that must not happen. Instead, both public and private leaders must recognize that necessity drives innovation. As Snobar analogizes, comfort breeds inertia; adversity forces reinvention. He recalls that "our home isn't burning, but we're certainly at threat of it." And that sharp sense of danger is pushing Canadians to think bigger about our future.

To capitalize on this crisis, leaders must unite all sectors around a shared vision. History shows this can work. After World War II, once-devastated Germany, Japan, and Korea convened governments, businesses, labour, and academia to ask what a prosperous future might look like. The result is decades of spectacular growth and innovation. Canada can have a similar story.

For this to happen, we need a national strategy that goes beyond letting the market sort itself out and cobbling together corporate bailouts. Industrial policy is not a dirty word if used to align resources with national ambition.

The current moment, which holds a mix of geopolitical uncertainty, technological change, and political division, may be Canada's closest thing to such a watershed. The country is more engaged than Hyder has seen in decades. "Canadians have always been more engaged in US politics than Canadian politics," he notes, but now "I can say it's the first time in my lifetime I've seen people more engaged in Canadian politics."

That energy creates an opening for leaders to inspire a new ambition. It means that the next national conversation is no longer confined to kitchen table worries about potholes and transit delays. It can include big questions about productivity, innovation, and intergenerational prosperity.

Hyder points out that voters never mention competitiveness or productivity to candidates, even though these are the issues on Canada's front burner. Until leaders start talking about long-term challenges, elections will yield short-sighted policies. Hyder warns: "If you talk potholes at the door, you get a pothole government." Leaders must educate the public, expand the political menu, and then act on that mandate.

In practice, leaders in government and business alike must step up. Hyder tells CEO colleagues bluntly that politicians, bureaucrats, and even teachers and doctors will not lead this push. *They* will. The public trusts business leaders to deliver results, he says, so CEOs have a duty to set an example. This means calling for higher standards and accountability within their industries and insisting on government policies that actually produce outcomes.

Leaders must also practise cultural humility and acceptance. We shouldn't celebrate tolerance that implies passivity, but acceptance and respect. "Don't talk about Canada as a tolerant society," Hyder says. "Tolerance is what you do when a baby is crying on a flight. Understanding why is different. Acceptance and understanding—that's what I'm after." Canadian leaders need to model a culture where diversity of backgrounds and thought is not just endured but actively embraced as a strength.

Leadership in Public and Private Sectors

Government leaders can create enabling conditions. They should set bold national goals (in areas such as cleantech, AI, or critical minerals) and use policy tools to make them happen. That means smarter procurement that champions Canadian innovators.

Hyder notes that public procurement is a huge lever. If governments deliberately buy Canadian technology, they grow domestic champions. He praises companies such as Bombardier and CAE—global leaders in aerospace—pointing out it's absurd that Canada doesn't insist on buying homegrown products. "We have a prime minister that doesn't even fly in a Canadian plane," he complains, highlighting how lax we've been about biasing our own industry. He suggests that Ottawa should emulate its Olympic playbook and invest real money in strategic industries, rather than spreading it evenly.

Hyder also reminds policymakers to judge by results, not just good intentions. He warns that in comfortable times, governments can craft elegantly written laws that fail in reality. For instance, when the Trudeau government passed Bill C-69 (energy regulation reform), it was certain it would lead to infrastructure projects, but this was not the case. "The measurement of public policy is not Parliament passing the bill. The measurement is, did the bill achieve its intended outcome?" That outcome-oriented mindset must drive leaders in Ottawa.

Corporate and civil leaders must match that drive. Many Canadian corporations still favour safe, incremental improvements over disruptive innovation. To change this, CEOs and board chairs should reward risk-taking internally. They can allocate budgets for moonshot projects and tolerate failure. Hyder emphasizes that, when complacency reigns, even business groups fall into endless debates over small things.

To break free, companies need a more combative spirit. We saw this when the government clamped down on domestic firms and Hyder's council fought to protect Canadian champions.

Leaders in the startup ecosystem also play a key role. Here, Snobar's experience at DMZ is instructive. He has transformed the incubator to focus not only on unicorn dreams but also on "vulnerable leadership" and inclusion. Early in the pandemic, DMZ threw out its old playbook and revamped programs to reach entrepreneurs left out of the tech boom. It launched specialized boot camps for women, a Black Innovation Summit, and even an angel investor initiative to get capital to underserved founders.

The message was that success must be shared. These efforts echo the theme that impolite Canadianness can mean defying conventional wisdom for the moral right. Snobar insists diversity and empathy are competitive advantages, as more perspectives mean more creative solutions.

Importantly, Snobar also uses leadership to build confidence in the Canadian ecosystem. He recently helped launch the Oh Canada Tech Directory: a curated list of Canadian startups, many already generating revenue, that buyers (including governments and global customers) can discover. He explains the rationale: After COVID-19 upended supply chains and trade assumptions, "Canadian companies can actually support Canadians … put Canadian technology at the highest pedestal … to allow great companies and great products … to shine."

It's an attempt to turn passive patriotism into active buying power. As he says, too many governments and big firms "have always been inclined to take on American technology. This doesn't mean American products are better, just more popular. We should stand up for ourselves." Changing this cultural habit requires leaders in business and government to look beyond perceived safety to reward and scale homegrown innovation.

Hyder likewise pushes businesses to serve as role models. He stresses mentorship and visibility. As a frequent media commentator and podcast host, he brings the successes and failures of Canadian leaders into public view. He is cochair of networks that advance women in leadership and guides policy from Ottawa to international forums. In short, he lives by the principle that leaders should show, not just tell. He tells young CEOs, "Don't wait for permission," and start doing the work of renewal.

Training, Mentorship, and Intergenerational Drive

A culture of ambition must be taught and reinforced. Formal leadership training and mentorship programs can cultivate the next generation of bold movers. Programs such as McKinsey's Generation, while not yet household names, aim to instill strategic vision and change-management skills in public servants. The private sector has its own accelerators that combine technical training with leadership coaching. But more should be done. Corporations could pair young managers with experienced mentors, and cross-sector fellowships could rotate promising talent through government, industry, and nonprofits.

Both Hyder and Snobar came from immigrant backgrounds, and they channel that perspective. Hyder recalls that, since he came from an immigrant family, even a strong work ethic became a liability. He says he was repeatedly told by colleagues, "You work too hard," as if ambition itself were suspicious. His advice from his father that you "have to want to be the best" stands in stark contrast to the "good enough" attitude he warns against.

Snobar's own journey was circuitous, with stops in military service, hotels, and academia until he found his purpose at DMZ.

It's a journey propelled by a desire to "return the debt" to Canada for giving him the opportunity. Immigrant and first-generation leaders often have that hunger, and Canada should leverage it.

Another source of ambition is generational vision. As Hyder points out, many Canadians want better lives for their children and grandchildren. *Will my economy grow? Will I have a pension? Will my kid get a job?* These are all questions people ask.

If leaders can frame their bold agendas in terms of improving the next generation's prospects, they tap into a powerful motive. For instance, the technology strategy can be pitched not just in GDP points but in terms of "jobs for our kids outside the basement." Leaders should remind Canadians that great projects today mean wealth and skills for tomorrow's adults.

To bridge generations, leaders can serve as mentors and role models. Policymakers might establish national youth councils for innovation, letting young entrepreneurs advise on funding and curriculum. Universities and foundations could expand internships that place students inside startups and policy labs. Perhaps most importantly, senior leaders should admit uncertainty and share their struggles.

Both Hyder and Snobar frequently speak candidly about fear and risk. That candour can encourage younger people to step up, seeing that even seasoned executives started with doubts. By engaging directly through podcasts, public forums, or classroom talks, Canada's leaders can ignite the innate ambition in the next generation.

Removing the Scaffolding: Overcoming Risk Aversion

A culture of ambition cannot grow under institutional fear. Too often, Canadian organizations, from governments to grant agencies, react to proposals with "Let's think about the downside" instead of "What's the upside?" Snobar calls out this reflex and says, "If there's no risk, there's no reward." Yet too many politicians are rewarded for taking "the safe bet."

One step is to reform incentives so that experimenting is encouraged. Grants and loans could, for example, explicitly include "rapid prototyping" clauses that fund early failures. Agile procurement policies (as Snobar advocates) could allow startups to pilot public projects with partial funding, subject to quick review. Government agencies might create internal venture units that operate like startups, taking small risks in exchange for potentially big returns.

At present, red tape often strangles innovation. Snobar points out a concrete example: Companies building prefabricated laneway houses can construct a home in a few weeks, but current regulations slow permits and on-site work to months. This is not a problem of technology but of political will. Bold leaders need to ask this: *If Dubai can turn sand into one of the world's most advanced cities in thirty years, why can't Toronto build faster than traditional contractors?* The answer lies in governance courage.

Many executives already embody this courage. The entrepreneurs Hyder interviews "explored the unexplored and embraced the unknown."[153] But governments must catch up. Snobar suggests looking abroad for models. In places such as Norway and the UAE, leadership is set up more like a corporation with clear targets and accountability. After discovering oil, Dubai's leaders didn't say, "We can't." They assembled talent, set aggressive goals, and professionalized the government to execute them. Canada could emulate parts of this by ensuring public servants are rewarded for achieving national metrics, not just for playing it safe.

Cultural incentives matter too, and Canada still lags in venture capital risk-taking. As recent business students at Ivey note, a "prevalent fear of failure" drives investors away, pushing Canadian founders to take their best ideas to Silicon Valley.[154] To counter this, public figures can praise failure as a learning step by celebrating companies that pivot out of unsuccessful bets. Awards, media stories, and public speeches can highlight entrepreneurs who took big chances, not just the ones who happened to win.

Finally, achieving this cultural shift requires humility from established leaders. Both Hyder and Snobar emphasize listening. Hyder admits that Canadians are right to expect more from their leaders. Snobar, likewise, avoids traditional posturing: He calls attention to his team's failures as well as successes, treating innovation as a collective journey.

When executives show vulnerability and admit that they don't know all the answers, it empowers others to speak up with ideas. Innovation thrives in a tolerant climate, and as Hyder argues, true tolerance in leadership is not mere lip service to diversity but respect and understanding for different approaches.

Looking Forward: A Bold Canadian Vision

Fostering a culture of ambition and innovation is a national project that requires both policy shifts and attitude changes. The task is to transform passive pride into the active pursuit of greatness. Leaders must set big goals, then mobilize whole sectors to reach them. Concretely, Canada needs to implement the following:

- **Visionary leadership:** Encourage CEOs, mayors, premiers, and cabinet ministers who articulate a daring goal and work relentlessly toward it. They should invoke the ethos of "If not us, who?" and rise to the challenge of this era.
- **Training and mentorship:** Expand leadership academies in both public and private domains. Pair experienced leaders with emerging talent. Encourage cross-sector secondments so innovators learn policymaking and policymakers learn innovation.
- **Risk-tolerant policies:** Reform procurement, taxation, and regulation to reward experimentation. Implement innovation sandboxes or pilot programs for new ideas (as Alberta has done for some fintech and insurance projects). Allow government contracts for early-stage firms under supervised trials. Create rapid-review units in agencies to handle novel proposals.
- **Immigrant and youth inclusion:** Ensure that leadership in boardrooms and legislatures reflects the country's diversity. Immigrant entrepreneurs bring global networks and fresh perspectives; youth bring digital-native insights and urgency. Cultivate programs that elevate leaders from all backgrounds. Hyder reminds us that we need the acceptance and understanding that comes from true inclusion.
- **Rewarding resilience:** Value businesses and projects that build slowly, survive downturns, and adapt, not just skyrocket and crash. Recognize that a resilient economy weathers shocks. Likewise, encourage employees to "learn in the sun and in the rain." Teach them to scale back when needed but never shut down operations entirely.

- **Accountability and metrics:** Set clear, outcome-oriented metrics for every initiative. Track not just inputs (funding, tax credits) but outputs (patents, companies, exports, social impact). Report progress transparently so citizens and businesses stay motivated.

This is, after all, a collective endeavour. Every Canadian has a role, whether as a consumer who chooses local innovations, an investor willing to fund dreams, a teacher inspiring entrepreneurship, or a voter demanding forward-thinking policies. The leadership doesn't only come from boardrooms or cabinet tables; it also comes from communities and individuals. As Hyder emphasizes, Canadians are not foolish. We are "a very smart group." Once leaders frame the debate, they trust citizens to answer it wisely.

In the end, fostering ambition means renewing our narrative as a nation. We must move from polite humility to what Snobar calls the "renewed pride and ambition" at the heart of being an impolite Canadian. We have seen glimpses of provinces and companies rethinking their roles in global supply chains and bold discussions of Canada's role on the world stage. Let's build on that momentum.

It feels like a once-in-a-generation opportunity. As Snobar says, Canada's house may not yet be on fire, but we feel the heat coming from outside. "Leadership is not a popularity contest ultimately," he reminds us. It's about doing the hard, unglamorous work today for a better tomorrow.

So, let's seize our own moment now, set higher goals, invest in talent, and take the risks. Canada has everything it needs—people, resources, values—but it needs leadership to unlock it. It's time to take down our fences of fear and aim for the sky.

"Canada must aim not just to participate in the global economy, but to lead in it."

—PAUL MARTIN (FORMER PRIME MINISTER OF CANADA)

CHAPTER 12

LET'S GO!

IN CIVIC CIRCLES, there's a saying that goes "No one is coming; it's up to us." This is a truth we have to actively embrace. Canada is not lacking in capability. We have talent. We have trust. We have institutional strength and global networks. What has been missing is the right mindset.

We are a G7 nation whose strength is not measured only by GDP but by the talent and diversity of our people. From the researchers in our universities to the entrepreneurs in small towns, Canadians have creativity and grit to share with the world.

We are rich in raw resources, yes, but our true wealth lies in human capital and the universities and startups that could tackle global challenges. Canadian research helped sequence one of the first cancer genomes and helped discover insulin, and our scientists often rank at the top in global innovation indices. If we shouted these achievements from the rooftops, eyes would widen around the world. Meanwhile, our cities consistently rank high in quality-of-life surveys. That's quietly grand, and people notice when we mention it.

The seeds of our future lie in the hands of every Canadian ready to act. Each person working abroad as a Canadian is a messenger of our values and skills. Thankfully, we have thousands of such ambassadors—students, engineers, entrepreneurs, and volunteers—carrying pieces of Canada from Buenos Aires to Beijing to Beirut. Imagine if each of us saw the world not as an ocean to divide us but as a chasm to cross.

The seeds of our future lie in the hands of every Canadian ready to act.

For every Canadian success we share, more opportunities spring up. We live in a world where news from Toronto can reach Nairobi and New Delhi in seconds. This connectivity is a signal, not a warning; it means our influence can be global and instantaneous. It shows we have the tools to make a difference—now we just need the will. The good news is that we already have four advantages to work with:

- **Diversity and talent:** Our people speak hundreds of languages and come from every continent. This global connection is a strategic asset.
- **Innovative spirit:** Canadians are creative builders. We excel in technology, arts, science, and social innovation.
- **Values as influence:** Compassion, fairness, democracy—our core values resonate worldwide. They give weight to our voice in international forums.

- **Networks and reach:** From diaspora communities to trade relations, Canada's footprint spans the globe. We need only broaden it with confidence.

Each of the strengths above can be turned into influence if we act. Our universities send thousands of graduates abroad; those alumni become bridges back to Canada's best ideas. If we invest in our people's connections and our leaders speak boldly about our contributions, Canada's untapped potential will surge forward. For every Canadian success story we tell, more doors open elsewhere. We have the tools to make a global impact. Now let's use them.

From Humility to Confidence

We also need self-confidence and a quiet cultural pride. As Global Executive Search specialist Alain Pescador[155] put it, "Ours is to be humble and polite." But he insists, "We need to have a shift in attitude if we want to advance the agenda of Canada." It's not arrogance he's calling for but balance.

Picture a Canadian ambassador at a global summit. They speak with kindness and courtesy, of course, but also with clear self-assurance. They remind others of Canada's legacy of peacekeeping, our leadership in clean energy, and the millions of lives we have helped change. They listen thoughtfully, but when stakes are high, they speak up to defend Canadian interests. This is the balance we seek: cultural humility and cultural confidence together.

As Canadians, oftentimes, we are too meek. We tend to let others take the lead. Canada has always recognized the North as important, but we only seem to take it seriously when the United States moves to assert control over the Arctic. "We seem to be bullied far too easily or, worse, too willing to sit back and let others set the course,"

Pescador warned, quoting a common refrain. When our politeness is a weakness, our interests can be overshadowed.

As a kid, I was taught to never brag about being Canadian—just do the work and not boast. That upbringing served me well in many ways, but in global settings, it can make us hesitate. We should teach the next generation a bit differently: to say "thank you" for acknowledging their work and then to describe with pride what Canada contributed to a global project.

This is a subtle yet important shift. We often apologize for things we should not. Imagine how powerful it would be to start saying, "Thank you, and here's what Canada is doing about it." I once watched a Canadian negotiator nod quietly while a stronger country made demands, and only later did he timidly raise a concern. What if he had spoken up firmly at the outset? We owe our representatives the backing to do just that.

Even outside politics, everyday Canadians can practise this. If a colleague or friend compliments your work, you can smile and say, "Thanks, I learned it in Canada." These little expressions teach confidence. It's OK to say "Canada" proudly. After all, we know we've earned our stripes in education, medicine, and peace. Why shouldn't everyone else hear it?

Telling Our Story Abroad

This confidence can start with storytelling. Each of us has a Canadian story worth sharing. Stories of ingenuity, of giving back, of crossing oceans to help others. These are powerful. A single story of a Canadian teacher in sub-Saharan Africa building a school can inspire millions and open doors. Yet, we often underplay our own narratives. We say, "Oh, I'm just a teacher" or "It was nothing."

It's time to tell these stories with pride.

Every Canadian travelling abroad carries a piece of our narrative: the laughter of our multicultural cities, the perseverance of our entrepreneurs, the kindness of our communities. Pescador points out that being truly proud of our diversity means more than lip service. Consider this: When a storm hit the Philippines, Canada quietly donated aid, but rarely do we broadcast those figures. Meanwhile, when Canada scores a goal in hockey, everyone knows. It can be reversed: World relief comes with a maple leaf logo. We have many humanitarian stories in Haiti, in Lebanon, and on the streets of Cairo with our engineers and doctors. Those are Canadian stories too, if we only choose to tell them.

And each time we broadcast one, the world remembers. Stories of Canadians shining in crisis or innovation are not boastful. They are invitations for others to collaborate. When someone hears that a Canadian doctor saved lives after an earthquake, it builds our collective brand. That story might inspire a donor in Germany to fund another Canadian-led program. You never know which connection will spark the next global breakthrough.

As Pescador notes, "No one likes just to be nice. People like to have some swag to them. And that's what we need." In other words, alongside our trademark kindness, we must carry confidence and a little pride. We can be our generous and humble selves yet still stand firm and share what makes us great.

The Boldness of the Impolite Canadian

To Pescador, being "impolite" on the world stage is simply being boldly Canadian. It means not shrinking from the spotlight. Politeness is still a virtue at home, he says, but abroad, we can add a dose of fearlessness.

This boldness calls for an unapologetic attitude when we present ourselves internationally, especially in business or diplomacy. A case in point is Jim Balsillie, the former co-CEO of BlackBerry. Balsillie was often criticized for his brash style, but he got results. He is not afraid to voice unpopular opinions, such as calling out Canada's political and business leaders for failing to protect our intellectual property. In his op-eds, he has argued that Canada must take a harder line to ensure innovations stay here with Canadian companies, rather than slipping away, as has too often been the case.

Interestingly, Pescador is Mexican by birth. Perhaps that mix of backgrounds helps him see that Canadians could borrow a bit of that fiery confidence. I think any Canadian could use some of that spirit. We should not view our own country as separate from the world's bold talk. We are here to join the conversation, not whisper on the sidelines.

It means taking action: opening new markets, leading initiatives on climate change, championing values we hold dear. In our own lives, it could mean setting a new example: a Canadian tech startup saying, "We will compete on fair terms" or a nonprofit saying, "We will advance reconciliation here and share what we learn abroad." These actions don't feel impolite in the aggressive sense. They feel necessary in a competitive world.

Breaking Barriers to Go Global

Of course, none of this change will happen without courage and conviction. Some Canadians face internal barriers. "I'm just a small-town kid, what can I do on the world stage?" they say. Others worry about going against the Canadian grain, afraid of seeming arrogant or aggressive. Those are mindsets we must dismantle. If one Canadian can start a tech company in Africa or lead a startup in Europe, then any of us can reach beyond the obvious opportunities at home.

Institutional barriers remain too. We have often been too insular. Think of how rare it is to send our business leaders or artists on global tours compared to some other countries. We talk of great plans, but sometimes those plans end up gathering dust. This time, let's follow through. Our future depends on concrete steps, not just speeches. When our policies align with our spirit, we'll see those results.

At 369 Global, alignment and taking action are core to our DNA. One way we are doing this is 369 Global's progress toward establishing "made in Canada" Global Skilling Centres. This model reimagines how Canada can expand its influence abroad while tackling urgent workforce shortages at home. It is an innovative approach to vocational education and training for in-demand professions. Rather than relying solely on immigration after arrival, these centres would deliver training in fields such as healthcare, business, and technology directly in overseas markets.

Our approach to global skilling partnerships is to ensure that Canadian standards and quality of vocational training help skill up for labour market gaps in origin countries, so there is truly a triple win: for Canada, for the source country, and, ultimately, for the skilled migrant. This made-in-Canada training is built around what labour markets and employers actually need, creating graduates who can strengthen their local economies back home or, down the road, come to Canada as immigrants whose skills already match available jobs.

The benefits are threefold. Canadian employers gain a dependable talent pipeline, prospective immigrants access affordable training that is relevant both in Canada and in their home countries, and Canada positions itself as a global leader in education and workforce development. With student visa numbers under scrutiny and critical labour shortages mounting, Global Skilling Centres would offer a fresh pathway, one that is proudly Canadian in design but global in reach. And with advocacy already underway at the federal level, this is not just an idea; it is a near-term opportunity to act boldly.[156]

Going global might also mean forging unexpected partnerships. Sure, Europe is a friend and Asia is booming, but what about Africa, Latin America, or the Middle East? We should not default to familiarity. We can use the ties in our great mosaic to reach places others overlook. It's about asking, "What can Canada offer them, and what can we learn in return?" For example, a Canadian engineer I met got his start in Nigeria because he learned Yoruba as a hobby. When a company in Lagos needed a bridge design, they trusted the Canadian who speaks Yoruba far more than any other foreigner. His Canadian roots made him relatable. That trust opened doors that no amount of formal pitching could. If each of us spoke at least one language of a trading partner, imagine the goodwill we'd earn!

Here are some ways Canadians can start breaking barriers today:

- **Travel with purpose:** Treat every trip abroad as a chance to exchange ideas, not just to take something. Bring Canadian ideas and curiosity wherever you go.
- **Connect our communities:** Help local businesses partner globally. If you run a nonprofit, find a sister organization in another country. If you teach, link your classroom with students overseas. These bridges make our reach wider.
- **Speak up about Canada:** When you meet someone from another country, share a Canadian success or value. Tell them what you love about Canada's innovation or culture. And be curious about theirs.

- **Empower our ambassadors:** Support cultural and educational exchange programs. Attend events where Canadians abroad share their stories. Urge our leaders to invest in the international plans they propose.
- **Invest in our future:** Encourage funding for programs that send young Canadians around the world as interns, researchers, or volunteers. The more we spread our energy globally, the more influence we build.

There are examples we can point to, such as a university in Nova Scotia partnering with a research centre in Vietnam to launch a joint aquaculture program. It began with simple conversations about marine science. "I heard Canadians excel in cold-water fisheries. Could we learn from each other?" From that, student exchanges and trade followed. A small question about Canada turned into opportunities for both nations. This is how one bridge was built by talking, teaching, and listening.

Each of these steps helps dismantle the mindset that keeps us small. We Canadians are comfortable with modesty, but let's not mistake modesty for mediocrity. We will never outgrow our potential if we insist on staying in the safe zone. To grow, we must believe we belong at the biggest tables and fights of our time.

A Call to Action

Canada has everything it takes to rise, but it will only happen if we choose to do it. I ask you again: *What will you do?* The world is listening, and there is a place for your voice. If each of us answers that call, we will light fires around the globe. I want you to put this book down and start acting. Yes, you.

As Pescador says, "The time is now; this is that moment for us as a country—and let's get to work." Each of us has a sphere of influence—our school, our workplace, our neighbourhood, our family—where we can make a difference. Plant the seeds of Canada's global future there.

Our strength starts at home, in the way we treat our neighbours, friends, and strangers. And make service beyond borders your mantra. Look up ways to use your skills and passions for others, whether it's mentoring someone in a faraway country online, donating expertise, or even moving across an ocean to help a new community.

What will you tell the world about Canada? Picture the day when a leader of another country asks, "Why did Canada step up on this issue?" We want to be able to answer this: "Because Canadians like you asked, and we had the courage and know-how to act."

For years, we said, "Maybe we should" or "It's not our turn." Now, let's say, "We will." It doesn't matter if you're a student, a teacher, a mechanic, or an artist—every role in Canada has a global twist. Try teaching your favourite hobby to someone from another culture or watch a foreign film and think about what it has in common with a Canadian story. Each small step is a collective stride.

So, let's do this together. Lean into the ambition I know you have. Build a network that stretches to all corners of the earth.

CONCLUSION

IF YOU HAVE read this far, you know by now that being *impolite* in the Canadian sense doesn't mean abandoning our values of respect and decency. It means harnessing our boldness, clarity, and conviction and carrying them forward with unapologetic purpose.

Imagine the Canada that could be: a nation that roars its ideals from the mountaintops, not one that whispers apologies from the sidelines. A Canada where our natural kindness is matched by unyielding courage to do what's right and ambitious. We envision a country that stands proudly on the world stage—not as an adjunct to someone else's power but as a leader in its own right.

We must demand boldness from our leaders and demonstrate boldness in our own civic lives. Let's insist on leaders who aren't afraid to break the mould of politeness when action is required, who will prioritize *doing what is right over what is easy*. But let's also remember that leadership isn't confined to Parliament or boardrooms. Leadership lives in our communities, in our classrooms, in our homes.

Yes, taking on this mantle of the impolite will not always be easy. There will be discomfort. After all, we are pushing against generations of ingrained politeness and a deep-seated desire not to offend. There will be moments when speaking up feels awkward, when taking a stand risks criticism or failure.

But think of the alternative: a Canada that drifts aimlessly, forever saying "sorry" to the world while others shape the future. We owe ourselves more than that. We owe future generations a country that doesn't shy away from greatness. Every time you choose to raise your voice instead of biting your tongue, every time you hold Canada to a higher standard, you set an example for those who follow.

Our children and grandchildren will inherit either the burdens of our timidity or the fruits of our courage. Let's make it the latter. Let them say that in our time, Canada woke up. That we found our backbone and our voice. That we stopped being content with good enough and began striving for greatness.

Our children and grandchildren will inherit either the burdens of our timidity or the fruits of our courage.

Be the impolite Canadian our future needs. Be the one who speaks up in the meeting when everyone else stays silent. Be the neighbour who rallies others to a cause. Be the student who questions outdated assumptions. Be the citizen who demands better—from our institutions, from our leaders, and from yourself. No more shrinking back. No more "Maybe later" or "Someone else will do it."

We will do it. You and I, *all of us together*, will do it. With every bold step we take, every convention we question, every dream we dare to pursue, we are writing the next chapter of Canada.

ABOUT THE AUTHOR

KUMARAN NADESAN is a first-generation Canadian of Tamil heritage, a strategic advisor, and a provocative new voice in the national conversation on identity, power, and purpose. As cofounder of 369 Global, he helps lead a portfolio of companies focused on skills training, media, and global talent mobility. Formerly a civil servant in the Ontario government, Kumaran brings a rare blend of public policy insight, business acumen, and community leadership to the challenges facing Canada today.

He has advised governments, corporations, and nonprofits across sectors and borders. Kumaran is deeply committed to unlocking the potential of people, systems, and nations. His sharp, unapologetic lens on Canada's global role—shaped by lived refugee and immigrant experience and grounded in pragmatic optimism—fuels his mission to help the country grow bolder.

Kumaran frequently comments on Canadian identity, civic leadership, and global issues. He holds a BA (Hons.) from the University of Toronto Scarborough and a graduate certificate in strategic public management from the Schulich School of Business, York University. He currently lives in Brampton, Ontario, with his wife and two children, who inspire him to build a Canada worthy of their future.

ACKNOWLEDGMENTS

THIS BOOK WOULD not exist without Muraly Srinarayanathas—my business partner, mentor, and dear friend. Muraly, you didn't just encourage me to write this book—you challenged me to. You saw the potential in an unapologetically bold Canadian voice, and you reminded me that it was my responsibility to use it. Your conviction, intellect, and relentless commitment to our shared vision made this book not only possible but necessary. Thank you for holding up a mirror when I needed clarity and for never letting me settle for anything less than honest, courageous truth.

To those who gave generously of their time, intellect, and insights—this book is as much yours as it is mine. Thank you for challenging my assumptions and for sharing your lived experiences with honesty and heart. Your stories, ideas, and criticisms shaped the architecture of this book in ways you may not even realize. You made it sharper. You made it braver. Thank you Amarnath Amarasingam, Daniel Bernhard, Garreth Bloor, Jim de Wilde, Goldy Hyder, Shamira Madhany, David McKinnon, Thi Be Nguyen, Alain Pescador, Mark Radha, Harroon Siddiqui, Janet Silver, Abdullah Snobar, John Stackhouse, Rohan Thiru, Victor T. Thomas, and Sugumar Vivekanandasothy. Last but not least, I'm deeply indebted to Anowa Quarcoo, my multifaceted Chief of Staff, who brought her brilliance, empathy, and invaluable insights as a third culture individual to this work—this book simply would not be what it is without her.

To the policymakers, business leaders, educators, community builders, and everyday Canadians I spoke with along the way, your passion for Canada's future reminded me that this country is still writing its own story. This book is one small part of that evolving narrative.

And to the quiet supporters—the ones who didn't ask for credit but offered time, feedback, or simply encouragement when I needed it most—thank you. Your faith carried me forward on the days when doubt tried to win.

This book was not written in solitude. It was born in conversation, in community, and in conviction. Thank you all for being part of that journey.

ENDNOTES

1 "BlackNorth Initiative Founder Wes Hall on the Pace of Progress," *Glory Media*, February 13, 2022, https://www.glory.media/blacknorth-initiative-wes-hall-progress/.

2 Eric Weiner, "Can Canada Teach the Rest of Us to Be Nicer?," *BBC*, March 19, 2015, https://www.bbc.com/travel/article/20150311-can-canada-teach-the-rest-of-us-to-be-nicer.

3 Catherine McIntyre, "Do Canadians Deserve Their Reputation for Being Nice?," *Maclean's*, June 28, 2017, https://macleans.ca/culture/do-canadians-deserve-their-reputation-for-being-nice/.

4 Ibid.

5 "We Are a Country of Accomplishments: Alex Trebek Praises Canada in Never-Before-Heard Acceptance Speech," *CBC Radio Q*, January 7, 2021, https://www.cbc.ca/radio/q/thursday-jan-7-2021-michie-mee-lang-lang-and-more-1.5863366/we-are-a-country-of-accomplishments-alex-trebek-praises-canada-in-never-before-heard-acceptance-speech-1.5863370.

6 "Canada in 2041: A Larger, More Diverse Population with Greater Differences Between Regions," Statistics Canada, September 8, 2022, https://www150.statcan.gc.ca/n1/daily-quotidien/220908/dq220908a-eng.htm.

7 Ibid.

8 Ibid.

9 Weiner, "Can Canada Teach the Rest?"

10 Glenda Luymes, "Federal Election Results Show an Urban–Rural Divide in B.C. Here's Why Some Political Scientists Are Worried," *Vancouver Sun*, May 3, 2025, https://vancouversun.com/news/federal_election/federal-election-results-urban-rural-divide-bc-why-it-matters.

11 "Data on Polling—45th General Election," Elections Canada, accessed May 27, 2025, https://www.elections.ca/content.aspx?section=med&document=ge45_advpol&lang=e.

12 Bill Brioux, "Top 10 Canadian Stars of Saturday Night Live," *brioux.tv*, February 16, 2025, https://brioux.tv/blog/2025/02/16/top-10-canadian-stars-of-saturday-night-live/.

13 Ryan Heath and Lauren Gardner, "U.N. Vote Deals Trudeau Embarrassing Defeat on World Stage," *POLITICO*, June 17, 2020, https://www.politico.com/news/2020/06/17/un-vote-deals-trudeau-embarrassing-defeat-on-world-stage-326617.

14 Jocelyn Coulon, *Canada Is Not Back: How Justin Trudeau Is in Over His Head on Foreign Policy* (Dundurn, 2018), Chapter 7, p. 111–112.

15 Solange Márquez Espinoza, "U.S.–Canada Ties May Face Even Bigger Trouble," *Americas Quarterly*, March 3, 2025, https://americasquarterly.org/article/u-s-canada-ties-may-face-even-bigger-trouble/.

16 Jeff Galloway and Mihai Lupescu, *Canada to Strengthen Ties with the Indo-Pacific Region and Beyond* (United States Department of Agriculture, 2023), https://apps.fas.usda.gov/newgainapi/api/Report/DownloadReportByFileName?fileName=Canada+to+Strengthen+Ties+with+the+Indo-Pacific+Region+and+Beyond_Ottawa_Canada_CA2023-0051.pdf.

17 Mary Halloran et al., "The White Paper Impulse: Reviewing Foreign Policy Under Trudeau and Clark," accessed March 10, 2025, https://www.cpsa-acsp.ca/papers-2005/Halloran.pdf.

18 *Canada's Competitiveness in Attracting Infrastructure Investment* (University of Calgary School of Public Policy, 2023), https://www.policyschool.ca/wp-content/uploads/2023/08/NC54-Cdn-Competitiveness-for-Infrastr-Investment-1.pdf.

19 "AltaLink Announces Completion of Acquisition by Berkshire Hathaway Energy," *AltaLink*, December 1, 2014, https://www.altalink.ca/news/news-releases/altalink-announces-completion-of-acquisition-by-berkshire-hathaway-energy/.

20 Yvonne Lau, "How Trump Could Turbocharge the Brain Drain from Canada," *Financial Post*, January 27, 2025, https://financialpost.com/technology/trump-turbocharge-canada-brain-drain.

21 Jeremy Shaki, "The Maple Tech Exit: Canada's Brain Drain Crisis," *TechTalent.ca*, November 17, 2023, https://techtalent.ca/the-maple-tech-exit-canadas-brain-drain-crisis/.

22 Sylvanus Kwaku Afesorgbor et al., "The U.S. Tariff Threat: How It Will Impact Different Products and Industries," *The Conversation*, February 2, 2025, https://theconversation.com/u-s-tariff-threat-how-it-will-impact-different-products-and-industries-248824.

23 Jeffrey W. Hornung, "Japan's Long-Awaited Return to Geopolitics," *Foreign Policy*, February 6, 2023, https://foreignpolicy.com/2023/02/06/japan-china-taiwan-russia-geopolitics-defense-security-strategy/.

24 Arlene Dickinson, "America is nice. It has a lot going for it. And for a long time, it has claimed to be the greatest country in the world. But let's look at what actually makes a country great. A great country is safe for its children. It's educated. It's healthy. It has a high quality of life, stunning natural beauty, and a global presence that matters. A great country isn't just a slogan—it's a way of life. And by every meaningful measure, Canada is that country," LinkedIn, accessed February 21, 2025, https://www.linkedin.com/posts/arlenedickinson_america-is-nice-it-has-a-lot-going-for-it-activity-7292727806084464640-856K.

25 "The People Behind the Universal Declaration of Human Rights," Canadian Museum for Human Rights, February 23, 2021, https://humanrights.ca/story/people-behind-universal-declaration-human-rights.

26 Laurence Brosseau and Michael Dewing, "Canadian Multiculturalism," Publication No. 2009-20-E (Library of Parliament, last modified January 3, 2018), https://lop.parl.ca/sites/PublicWebsite/default/en_CA/ResearchPublications/200920E.

27 Krista McFadyen, "An Aboriginal Perspective on Canada's Human Rights 'Culture,'" *University of Alberta*, accessed March 11, 2025, https://scispace.com/pdf/an-aboriginal-perspective-on-canada-s-human-rights-culture-2m9ivuo2zv.pdf.

28 "First Nations Peoples and the Right to Vote Case Study," Elections Canada, accessed March 11, 2025, https://electionsanddemocracy.ca/voting-rights-through-time-0/first-nations-and-right-vote-case-study.

29 "The Residential School System National Historic Event," Government of Canada, last modified September 29, 2025, https://parks.canada.ca/culture/designation/evenement-event/sys-pensionnats-residential-school-sys.

30 "Residential School History," National Centre for Truth and Reconciliation, accessed March 11, 2025, https://nctr.ca/education/teaching-resources/residential-school-history/.

31 "QS World University Rankings 2024: Top Global Universities," Top Universities, accessed March 29, 2025, https://www.topuniversities.com/university-rankings/world-university-rankings/2024.

32 "Over Half of the International Students Struggle with Housing in Canada," *The Economic Times*, last modified February 4, 2025, https://economictimes.indiatimes.com/nri/study/over-half-of-the-international-students-struggle-with-housing-in-canada/articleshow/117906229.cms.

33 "Troop and Police Contributors," United Nations Peacekeeping, accessed March 29, 2025, https://peacekeeping.un.org/en/troop-and-police-contributors.

34 Dani-Elle Dubé, "Canada 150: 6 Canadian Stereotypes That Happen to Be True," *Global News*, June 28, 2017, https://globalnews.ca/news/3550982/canada-150-6-canadian-stereotypes-that-happen-to-be-true/.

35 Asheesh Moosapeta, "Canada Ranked Happiest Country in the G7," *CIC News*, March 22, 2025, https://www.cicnews.com/2025/03/canada-ranks-happiest-country-in-the-g7-0353149.html.

36 "Canada Ranked as 2nd Best Country Globally in 2023," *NewToBC*, October 17, 2023, https://newtobc.ca/news-and-events/news/canada-ranked-as-2nd-best-country-globally-in-2023/.

37 Canada Artificial Intelligence Strategy and Opportunities," International Trade Administration, "September 27, 2024, https://www.trade.gov/market-intelligence/canada-artificial-intelligence-strategy-and-opportunities.

38 Ibid.

39 Perspective Staff, "Canadian City Ranks Top 5 in the AI Revolution," *Perspective*, July 21, 2025, https://perspective.ca/toronto-ai-tech-talent/.

40 "Canada Ranked 2nd Globally on 2024 Cleantech Innovation Index," Canada Action, accessed March 11, 2025, https://www.canadaaction.ca/cleantech-innovation-index-ranking.

41 *A Mandate to Innovate.* Council of Canadian Innovators, May 6, 2025. https://www.canadianinnovators.org/content/a-mandate-to-innovate.

42 Izabela Shubair, "The Growth of Biotechnology in Toronto and Its Potential to Change Lives," Northeastern University—Toronto News & Events, August 19, 2024, https://toronto.northeastern.edu/the-growth-of-biotechnology-in-toronto/.

43 *Labour Force Survey, July 2022,* Statistics Canada, August 5, 2022, https://www150.statcan.gc.ca/n1/daily-quotidien/220805/dq220805a-eng.htm.

44 "Canada Leads Tech Talent Growth, Toronto Makes a Comeback," *CBRE*, September 18, 2024, https://www.cbre.ca/insights/articles/canada-leads-tech-talent-growth-toronto-makes-a-comeback.

45 Ibid.

46 "Spotlight: Capital Exited in Canadian Venture over the Past Decade," *RBCX*, November 13, 2024, https://www.rbcx.com/ideas/startup-insights/spotlight-capital-exited-in-canadian-venture-over-the-past-decade/.

47 "2023 Mercer Cost of Living Survey," Mercer, accessed March 11, 2025, https://www.mercer.com/en-ca/about/newsroom/cost-of-living-in-canada-2023/.

48 Ibid.

49 Michelle Butterfield, "We're No. 1! Canada Claims the Most Top 10 Liveable Cities in the World," *Global News*, June 23, 2023, https://globalnews.ca/news/9787103/canada-most-liveable-cities-top-10-2023/.

50 I should note this point might be argued by those who work on affordability issues.

51 "Canada: Overview of the Education System," OECD, accessed March 11, 2025, https://gpseducation.oecd.org/CountryProfile?primaryCountry=CAN&treshold=10&topic=EO.

52 "Immigration and Ethnocultural Diversity Statistics," Statistics Canada, accessed March 11, 2025, https://www.statcan.gc.ca/en/subjects-start/immigration_and_ethnocultural_diversity.

53 This will change for the next couple of years, as immigration numbers are being reduced to address affordability issues given housing shortages and not enough resources to address the increased demand on healthcare services.

54 "Canada Welcomes Historic Number of Newcomers in 2022," Government of Canada, accessed March 11, 2025, https://www.canada.ca/en/immigration-refugees-citizenship/news/2022/12/canada-welcomes-historic-number-of-newcomers-in-2022.html.

55 Ibid.

56 Peter Burgess, "Political Leadership—Tommy Douglas," *TrueValueMetrics*, accessed March 29, 2025, https://www.truevaluemetrics.org/DBadmin/DBtxt003.php?vv1=txt00018143#:~:text=Despite%20these%20qualifications%2C%20Douglas%20was,see%20Saskatchewan%20Doctors%E2%80%99%20Strike.

57 Ashifa Kassam, "Civil Rights Pioneer Viola Desmond Is First Woman on Canadian Currency," *The Guardian*, March 9, 2018, https://www.theguardian.com/world/2018/mar/09/civil-rights-pioneer-viola-desmond-is-first-woman-on-canadian-currency.

58 Craig Turner, "From the Archives: Charismatic, Controversial Ex-Canadian PM Pierre Trudeau Dies: 'He Was Towering in the Way FDR Was Towering,'" *Los Angeles Times*, September 29, 2000, https://www.latimes.com/local/obituaries/la-fg-former-canadian-premier-pierre-trudeau-dies-20000929-story.html.

59 James Tobin, "Queen of the Hurricanes," *Michigan Today*, July 5, 2018, https://michigantoday.umich.edu/2018/07/05/queen-of-the-hurricanes.

60 Ibid.

61 Ibid.

62 Justus Becker, "Geoffrey Hinton and the Dark Side of AI: Why the Father of Artificial Intelligence Is Worried," *AlphaAvenue Magazine*, August 21, 2024, https://alphaavenue.ai/en/magazine/technologies/geoffrey-hinton-and-the-dark-side-of-ai-why-the-father-of-artificial-intelligence-is-worried.

63 Timothy B. Lee, "Why the Deep Learning Boom Caught Almost Everyone by Surprise," *Understanding AI*, November 5, 2024, https://www.understandingai.org/p/why-the-deep-learning-boom-caught.

64 Josh Taylor and Alex Hern, "'Godfather of AI' Geoffrey Hinton Quits Google and Warns over Dangers of Misinformation," *The Guardian*, May 2, 2023, https://www.theguardian.com/technology/2023/may/02/geoffrey-hinton-godfather-of-ai-quits-google-warns-dangers-of-machine-learning.

65 Jackie Marchildon, "10 Times Canadian Leaders Inspired Us to Be Global Citizens," *Global Citizen*, May 24, 2017, https://www.globalcitizen.org/en/content/quotes-from-canadian-leaders/.

66 "Bob Rae Quotes," *Goodreads*, accessed March 14, 2025, https://www.goodreads.com/author/quotes/220947.Bob_Rae.

67 Marchildon, "10 Times Canadian Leaders Inspired."

68 Gunness & Associates, "Immigration Is the Primary Source of Canada's Labor Force Growth," accessed March 17, 2025, https://immigrationmatters.info/immigration-is-the-primary-source-of-canadas-labor-force-growth/.

69 *Canada's State of Trade 2025: Small and Medium Enterprises Taking On the Export Challenge* (Government of Canada, 2025), https://international.canada.ca/en/global-affairs/corporate/reports/chief-economist/state-trade/2025.

70 *Immigrant-Led Small and Medium-Sized Enterprise Exporters in Canada* (Government of Canada, last modified February 2021), https://www.international.gc.ca/trade-commerce/inclusive_trade-commerce_inclusif/sme-exporter-pme-exportatrice.aspx?lang=eng.

71 Ravi Jain, "The Role of Immigrants in Canada's Tech Sector," *Jain Immigration Law*, November 4, 2024, https://jainimmigrationlaw.com/the-role-of-immigrants-in-canadas-tech-sector/.

72 Julia Hornstein, "How Immigration Has Benefitted Canadian Sectors," *CIC News*, November 12, 2023, https://www.cicnews.com/2023/11/how-immigration-has-benefitted-canadian-sectors-1139585.html.

73 Ryan Fernandes, "International Students Contributed $30.9B to Canada's GDP in 2022," *Canada Immigration*, August 2, 2024, https://canadaimmigration.news/international-students-contributed-30-9b-to-canadas-gdp-in-2022/.

74 Helen Lowe, "Thoughts on a Book Quote by Margaret Atwood," *Helen Lowe Official Blog*, February 13, 2023, http://helenlowe.info/blog/2023/02/13/thoughts-on-a-book-quote-by-margaret-atwood/.

75 "Robertson Davies Quotes," *AzQuotes*, accessed March 17, 2025, https://www.azquotes.com/author/3693-Robertson_Davies.

76 "Sinead Bovell," *The Spotlight Agency*, accessed May 6, 2025, https://www.thespotlightagency.com/talent/sinead-bovell/.

77 Takara Small, "Model-Turned-Tech Founder Sinead Bovell on Why the Future of Tech Must Be Global," *3 Magazine*, March 3, 2025, https://threemagazine.com/culture/model-turned-tech-founder-sinead-bovell-on-why-the-future-of-tech-must-be-global/.

78 "Sinead Bovell," *The Spotlight Agency*.

79 "International Report Warns Against Loss of Control over AI," *Tech Xplore*, February 6, 2025, https://techxplore.com/news/2025-02-international-loss-ai.html.

80 Ibid.

81 Elisa Shoenberger, "The Bittersweet Story of Peace by Chocolate," *The Chocolate Professor*, January 31, 2024, https://www.thechocolateprofessor.com/blog/peace-by-chocolate.

82 Yoonji Han, "Simu Liu Claps Back at 'Trashest Take' That He Gets the 'Bulk' of Asian Male Roles in Hollywood: 'Way to Put Us Against One Another,'" *Business Insider*, May 5, 2023, https://www.businessinsider.com/simu-liu-huffpost-asian-representation-hollywood-diversity-2023-5.

83 Chris Halef, "Halifax Pop Explosion's Organizers Apologize to Performer for Volunteer's 'Overtly Racist' Actions," *CityNews Halifax*, October 26, 2017, https://halifax.citynews.ca/2017/10/26/halifax-pop-explosions-organizers-apologize-to-performer-for-volunteers-overtly-racist-actions-750282/.

84 Ibid.

85 Karen Thomas, "Autumn Peltier: A Long Walk for First Nations' Water Rights," *The Environment* (CIWEM), accessed May 6, 2025, https://www.ciwem.org/the-environment/autumn-peltier-a-long-walk-for-first-nations%E2%80%99-water-rights.

86 Ibid.

87 Autumn Peltier, "My Water Message for the World," *Rematriation*, March 8, 2021, https://rematriation.com/my-water-message-for-the-world/.

88 "Immigration, Place of Birth, and Citizenship—2021 Census Promotional Material," Statistics Canada, last modified October 26, 2022, https://www.statcan.gc.ca/en/census/census-engagement/community-supporter/immigration.

89 Ibid.

90 John Stackhouse, *Planet Canada: How Our Expats Are Shaping the Future* (Random House of Canada, 2020), 3.

91 Ibid.

92 Ibid.

93 Ibid.

94 Ibid.

95 Lucia Kovacikova, *Canadians Abroad: Overview of Recent Research and Implications for Public Policy* (McGill Institute for the Study of Canada, 2021), https://senatoryuenpauwoo.ca/media/wyzltmzl/canadians-abroad-report-en.pdf.

96 John Stackhouse, "Expats: A Secret Weapon Waiting to Be Discovered," *Diplomat*, April 2021, https://diplomatonline.com/mag/2021/04/expats-a-secret-weapon-waiting-to-be-discovered.

97 "Introducing 3, the New Magazine for Canadian Newcomers from SJC and 369 Global," Global 369, April 9, 2024, https://muralys.com/features/introducing-3-the-new-magazine-for-canadian-newcomers-from-sjc-and-369-global/#:~:text=curious%20alike%2C%20a%20testament%20to,the%20experiences%20of%20numerous%20others.

98 "Munnetram Featuring Kumaran Nadesan," Canadian Tamil Professionals Association, September 2020, https://tamilprofessional.ca/2020/09/munnetram-kumaran-nadesan/#:~:text=The%20first%20was%20when%20he%2C,donate%20tens%20of%20thousands%20of.

99 Ibid.

100 Kovacikova, *Canadians Abroad.*

101 Kovacikova, *Canadians Abroad.*

102 Jennifer Welsh, "Our Overlooked Diaspora," *Literary Review of Canada*, March 2011, https://reviewcanada.ca/magazine/2011/03/our-overlooked-diaspora/#:~:text=Hong%20Kong%20is%20another%20jurisdiction,The%20Canadian%20Chamber%20of.

103 Paul Samson and Nikolina Zivkovic, "Canada's Uncertain Future in a Multipolar World," *Centre for International Governance Innovation*, April 17, 2024, https://www.cigionline.org/articles/canadas-uncertain-future-in-a-multipolar-world/.

104 Severin de Wit, "Why Isn't Europe Embracing Canada as a Stronger Partner?," *LinkedIn*, March 15, 2025, https://www.linkedin.com/pulse/why-isnt-europe-embracing-canada-stronger-partner-severin-de-wit-kvnye.

105 Daniel Korski, "Partners in Decline," *European Council on Foreign Relations*, March 3, 2010, https://ecfr.eu/article/commentary_partners_in_decline_daniel_korski/.

106 Frank Hoffer, "The Transatlantic Alliance Is Dying—What Comes Next for Europe?," *Social Europe*, February 19, 2025, https://www.socialeurope.eu/the-transatlantic-alliance-is-dying-what-comes-next-for-europe.

107 Victor Thomas, interview by Ezra Byer, April 23, 2025, for *The Impolite Canadian*.

108 "India-Canada Relations: News & Updates," *Strategic Front*, accessed August 28, 2022, https://www.strategicfront.org/forums/threads/india-canada-relations-news-updates.3703/page-2.

109 Thi Be Nguyen, interview by Ezra Byer for *The Impolite Canadian*, May 7, 2025.

110 Wes J. Bryant, "When a CEO Plays President: Musk, Starlink, and the War in Ukraine," *Irregular Warfare Initiative*, October 17, 2023, https://irregularwarfare.org/articles/when-a-ceo-plays-president-musk-starlink-and-the-war-in-ukraine.

111 Leyland Cecco, "Canada's Failed UN Security Council Bid Exposes Trudeau's 'Dilettante' Foreign Policy," *The Guardian*, June 18, 2020, https://www.theguardian.com/world/2020/jun/18/canada-loses-bid-un-security-council-seat-justin-trudeau.

112 John Ralston Saul, *A Fair Country: Telling Truths About Canada* (Penguin Canada, 2009), Kindle edition, 11.

113 Ibid, 31.

114 Louise Blais, "Canadian Diplomacy Needs to Find Its Way Back from the Wilderness," *Policy Options*, September 11, 2023, https://policyoptions.irpp.org/magazines/september-2023/canadian-diplomacy-back-from-wilderness/.

115 Amarnath Amarasingam, interview by Ezra Byer, April 30, 2025, for *The Impolite Canadian.*

116 David Ljunggren et al., "A Canadian Tweet in a Saudi King's Court Crosses a Red Line," *Reuters,* August 10, 2018, https://www.reuters.com/article/world/a-canadian-tweet-in-a-saudi-kings-court-crosses-a-red-line-idUSKBN1KV2FO.

117 Muraly Srinarayanathas, interview by Ezra Byer, April 21, 2025, for *The Impolite Canadian.*

118 Jasmina Kelemen, "Canada H2 Sees Opening as Political Chaos Engulfs US," *Argus,* April 25, 2025, https://www.argusmedia.com/en/news-and-insights/latest-market-news/2682278-canada-h2-sees-opening-as-political-chaos-engulfs-us.

119 "Poilievre Pushes for National Projects: Another Bold Vision or a Desperate Bid to Stay Relevant?," *The Economic Times*, last modified June 10, 2025, https://economictimes.indiatimes.com/news/international/canada/poilievre-pushes-for-national-projects-another-bold-vision-or-a-desperate-bid-to-stay-relevant/articleshow/121746192.cms?from=mdr.

120 Levon Sevunts, "Liberals Bolster NAFTA Team, Reach Out to Former Foes for Advice," *Radio Canada International*, last modified August 4, 2017, https://www.rcinet.ca/en/2017/08/02/liberals-bolster-nafta-team-reach-out-to-for-former-foes-for-advice/.

121 Isaac Callan and Colin D'Mello, "Ontario and Alberta Sign Agreements to Study New Pipeline, Railway Projects," *Global News*, last modified July 7, 2025, https://globalnews.ca/news/11277819/danielle-smith-doug-ford-sign-agreements-in-calgary/#:~:text=their%20alignment%20on%20energy%20exports.

122 Ibid.

123 Ibid.

124 Kanishka Singh, "Canada Lawmakers Vote Unanimously to Label Russia's Acts in Ukraine as 'Genocide,'" *Reuters*, April 27, 2022, https://www.reuters.com/world/canada-lawmakers-vote-unanimously-label-russias-acts-ukraine-genocide-2022-04-27/.

125 Shamira Madhany, interview by Ezra Byer, April 30, 2025, for *The Impolite Canadian.*

126 "*Mandate Letter from the Prime Minister to the Cabinet,*" Office of the Prime Minister of Canada, May 21, 2025, https://www.pm.gc.ca/en/mandate-letters/2025/05/21/mandate-letter.

127 "Building Canada Strong: A Bold, Ambitious Plan for Our Future," Government of Canada, last modified May 27, 2025, https://www.canada.ca/en/privy-council/campaigns/speech-throne/2025/building-canada-strong.html.

128 Office of the Prime Minister, "*Mandate Letter.*"

129 Government of Canada, "*Building Canada Strong.*"

130 Creso Sá, "Canada Must Be More Audacious with Efforts to Attract Global Talent," *Policy Options*, April 18, 2024, https://policyoptions.irpp.org/magazines/april-2024/global-talent-chase/.

131 Rohan Thiru, interview by Ezra Byer for *The Impolite Canadian*, April 14, 2025.

132 Ibid.

133 Ibid.

134 *Canada's State of Trade 2023: Inclusive Trade* (Government of Canada, 2023), https://international.canada.ca/en/global-affairs/corporate/transparency/reports-publications/chief-economist/state-trade/2023.

135 Office of the Prime Minister, "*Mandate Letter.*"

136 Ibid.

137 Ibid.

138 Nanaki Vij, "Key Insights from Canada's Speech from the Throne," *Clear Blue Markets*, June 2, 2025, https://www.clearbluemarkets.com/knowledge-base/key-insights-from-canadas-speech-from-the-throne.

139 TC Energy, "TC Energy Announces Canada's Largest Indigenous Equity Ownership Agreement," news release, July 30, 2024, https://www.tcenergy.com/announcements/2024/2024-07-30-tc-energy-announces-canadas-largest-indigenous-equity-ownership-agreement/.

140 Ibid.

141 Vij, "Key Insights."

142 Government of Canada, "*Building Canada Strong.*"

143 Office of the Prime Minister, "*Mandate Letter.*"

144 Government of Canada, "*Building Canada Strong.*"

145 Government of Canada, *Canada's State of Trade 2023.*

146 Ibid.

147 Office of the Prime Minister, "*Mandate Letter.*"

148 TC Energy, "Equity Ownership Agreement."

149 Government of Canada, "*Building Canada Strong.*"

150 Office of the Prime Minister, "*Mandate Letter.*"

151 Goldy Hyder, interview by Kumaran Nadesan, April 15, 2025, for *The Impolite Canadian.*

152 Abdullah Snobar, interview by Ezra Byer, April 15, 2025, for *The Impolite Canadian.*

153 Camille Gilbert and Nicole Tessier, "Embracing Risk, Adaptability, and Action for Canada's Business Landscape," *Ivey Business School,* November 29, 2023, https://www.ivey.uwo.ca/news/blogs/2023/november/embracing-risk-adaptability-and-action-for-canadas-business-landscape/#:~:text=outcomes,unexplored%20and%20embraced%20the%20unknown.

154 Gilbert and Tessier, "Embracing Risk."

155 Alain Pescador, interview by Ezra Byer, May 5, 2025, for *The Impolite Canadian.*

156 369 Global, *Global Skilling for National Gain: Reimagining Canada's Talent Immigration Pipeline* (369 Global, June 18, 2025), https://www.369global.com/wp-content/uploads/2025/08/PolicyBrief-GlobalSkillingCentres-369Global-18JUN25copy-compressed.pdf.

MY IMPOLITE IDEAS FOR A BOLDER CANADA

In these pages, consider writing down your own impolite ideas for how to build a bolder and more impactful Canada. I would love to hear some of your ideas, which you can submit online at www.theimpolitecanadian.ca.